NOW A MAJOR
MOTION PICTURE

At theaters everywhere across the country, audiences have responded with a thunderous reaction to the film, *Walking Tall*. Why?

Because it isn't "just a movie," just as this isn't "just a book." It is truth, a truth we sometimes lose sight of, that one man, walking tall, unafraid, can do something—fight the system, improve his world, even at tremendous cost to himself and to his family.

It is the deeply moving, contemporary story of Buford Pusser, who wouldn't surrender to corruption and greed . . . and the woman who stood beside him until they killed her.

Buford Pusser is a real man who has both won and lost, but is still walking tall: his life has transcended the most exciting of suspense novels, his movie has caused people to stand up and applaud.

You won't be the same after you read his story.

WALKING TALL

by
Doug Warren

PINNACLE BOOKS • NEW YORK CITY

WALKING TALL

A Pinnacle Books original, published for the first time anywhere.

Based on the life story of Buford Pusser and the
motion picture, *Walking Tall.*

ISBN: 0-523-00478-8

First printing, September 1973
Second printing, October 1973
Third printing, November 1973
Fourth printing, January 1974
Fifth printing, May 1974
Sixth printing, July 1974
Seventh printing, September 1974

Printed in the United States of America

PINNACLE BOOKS, INC.
275 Madison Avenue
New York, N.Y. 10016

Contents

WALKING
TALL

Chapter One

"The Wild Bull" Returns

Impatient determination was a built-in characteristic of Buford Pusser; one that he and those around him had learned to live with. Once he started something there was no rest until the job was done, and he was no different when it came to traveling. They could easily have completed the trip the night before, and with the destination so attainable, Buford was mightily tempted. But on this occasion, despite all inner urgings to the contrary, he relented. They spent the night at a small motel less than a two-hour drive from home.

He knew without asking that this was the way Pauline wanted it. The children would have rest, and she could be sure they would be sparkling clean for the long-awaited reunion with their grandparents. There was also the dual consideration of Pauline's own quiet vanity. She too would want to look and feel her best for the first day of their new way of life.

Their car was a late model station wagon, but its vintage was obscured by the mud and dust of seven states. Even Buford's bold trademark on the side of the aluminum travel trailer was difficult to make out. The muscled arm with clenched fist could be seen, but the lettering beneath it: "BUFORD THE WILD BULL," was almost totally covered.

Their speed had slowed considerably as he maneuvered the trailer through the frequent curves and dips on the outer fringes of McNairy

County, but it made for a leisurely homestretch. When they passed the county corporation limits, Pauline nestled closer to her husband. She gave him an impulsive kiss on the cheek.

He grinned as his giant palm squeezed her thigh. "Watch out," he warned with a glance, "or I might get the idea you like me or something."

"Wouldn't want that to happen," she laughed in reply. Then, in a whisper beyond range of back seat eavesdroppers: "The word is *love*."

Buford had never wavered in his admiration of Pauline's refreshing beauty. She was in her late twenties, but looked younger. He supposed her willowy figure and youthful enthusiasm had a lot to do with it. Today she wore a crisp white blouse with a cotton skirt of red and white print. She wore her hand-tooled leather sandals, a Mayan necklace, and an ornately cast jangle bracelet. Her long chestnut hair was drawn into a pony-tail with a bright red and blue scarf.

Dwana, their pig-tailed six-year-old, poked her head over the front seat. "How much further, Daddy?" she asked, breaking up the smooching session. The question was being asked for perhaps the ten thousandth time in the past three days.

"*I* know," said Mike, showing off his superior knowledge from a two year age advantage. "I betcha we'll be at Grandpa's within half-an-hour."

"What makes *you* so smart?" said Buford, glancing amiably at his son through the rear-view mirror.

"The bridge," said Mike. He pushed his straight blond hair out of his eyes as they crossed a steel-framed bridge, canopied by willow trees. "I remember this bridge from last time."

"You have a good memory, son," Buford said. "In just a little while we'll be—home."

Buford couldn't express the excitement he was feeling at the moment, so he didn't try. But there was always a surge of deep emotion when he returned to these lush, green hills of home. He loved Selmer and all of McNairy County and thought of it often. It was the place where he was born, where he phrased his first words, where he learned the feeling of pleasant exhaustion at the end of a hard day's work. It was in Selmer, also, where he had his first sweet taste of success in athletics, where he felt he was best among many.

"I wish I'd taken the time to get the car and trailer washed," Buford said, his thoughts projecting to the imminent reunion. "We must look like a band of wandering gypsies."

Pauline had a musical laugh. She offered it now in response to Buford's remark. "If all that mud and dust says we're gypsies, then it's telling the real truth."

"Nope," he said with his strong jaw set in determination. "We were *once* . . . but not any more."

"That's music to my ears, Buford," she said. "Pure and beautiful music."

In a few minutes, the caravan slowed to make its turn from the county highway into a lane of red clay. The car and trailer groaned and creaked along the narrow roadway, full of bumps and dips from many years traffic of trucks and other farm vehicles.

11

After passing a long line of oaks and maples, there was a sharp turn in the road. When the car headed out of the turn the Pusser farmhouse came into view. It was a large, three-storied structure of gleaming white clapboard. It had a pillared porch and rococo trim, typical of houses of the post–Civil War era.

"There's Grandpa!" Mike shouted. "I see him."

Buford saw his father at the same moment. He and two hired hands were rolling lengths of logging chain next to a flatbed truck. They were between the house and the brick barn, in a yard cluttered with tools of a farmer's trade: two trucks, a tractor, a plow, and a cultivator. Buford rolled into the driveway with triumphant blasts of his horn.

Almost simultaneously with the sound of the horn, the front door opened and Grandma appeared, her face beaming. She dried her hands on her ever-present apron and hurried down the porch steps toward her returning family. Grandpa dropped the length of chain, and started from the barn, taking swipes at his weathered cheeks with a blue and white bandana.

The excitement of the reunion extended even to Shep, the family dog. He ran in circles barking as Dwana ran to Grandma's waiting arms. Mike was on his way to meet his grandfather. "Grandpa, Grandpa!" Mike screamed. "We're going to have a house that doesn't move!"

"Just like real people," Dwana joined in. "Aren't we, dad?"

"That's right," said Buford over the warm

handshake with his father. "A regular house with a solid foundation."

"Where?" said Grandpa, with the lines of his bronzed face set in a grin.

"Right around here somewhere," said Buford. "That is, if you can tolerate us."

Grandma released Dwana to give Pauline a motherly hug. "Oh, Pauline . . . is it true?"

"It is, Grandma," Pauline said.

Eyeing Buford suspiciously, Grandpa said, "Don't tell me you're givin' up wrestling?"

This was an announcement Pauline just had to make herself. "Yes, Grandpa," she said proudly. "Buford the Bull is officially retired from the ring."

Overwhelmed by the good news, Grandma went to Buford. "Oh, son, I'm so happy. You don't know how many nights I lay awake wonderin' if you'd get hurt."

"*Daddy* get hurt?" Mike said in disbelief.

Buford laughed as he hugged his mother. "You should have been worrying about the other guys."

'By God!" said Grandpa, "this calls for a drink!"

"With you," said Grandma, chiding pleasantly, "just about *everything* calls for a drink."

"When a man's son finally comes to his senses, it's celebratin' time," said Grandpa. He turned to Pauline. "Bet you had something to do with this."

"It was Buford's decision as always," said Pauline. "I just agreed . . . *immediately*."

Laughter accompanied them as they headed toward the house. Buford lingered a step behind the others with Grandpa. "It was a street going nowhere, dad," Buford said solemnly. "Organized dishonesty . . . the system. You could only win when *they* said so, climb the ladder when they *let* you, breathe when *they* felt like giving you air." Buford started to get heated. "I just got fed up with other people running my life their way, and. . . ."

Pauline paused to touch his arm. "Buford . . . it's all over now," she said soothingly. "Don't relive it. They weren't worth it."

Grandma moved in. "See what you did with your fool questions?" The scolding was aimed at Grandpa. "They've come home. Nothin' else is important."

Buford reached out his arm and pulled Pauline to his side. His anger was a thing of the past. "Don't worry," he said to Grandma. "I'm not fighting *anybody* anymore . . . Buford's word."

With initial greetings out of the way, Dwana's interest was aimed at the barn. "I want to go see the cows!"

"That's for first-graders," her brother teased. "I want to go see dad's solid gold football."

The adults watched happily as the children went off on their separate adventures, and then moved inside.

Grandma and Pauline went to the kitchen to begin preparing a farmer's noontime feast, and Grandpa reluctantly rejoined his men in the farmyard. Buford promised to join him in a few minutes, but he couldn't delay his visit to the room upstairs. He wanted to be with Mike as he explored the trophies of the past.

This would be the room where he and Pauline would sleep, so Buford carried the heavy suitcases with him on the climb up the banistered stairway. Buford didn't give it a second thought, but he carried in a single trip what had taken a bellhop at a recent stopover *three* trips to carry.

The gleaming white walls of the wood-paneled bedroom were spotless, with not a grain of dust to be found. He wondered then if his mother dusted every deer head, mounted catfish, and the dozens of trophies every day of her life. He imagined she had.

Mike stared with awe in front of the table on which was displayed the golden football. "State Champion," the engraving said, "High School All American." Buford deposited the luggage near the door and went to his son. He put a massive hand around Mike's shoulder. "You never forgot that football," said Buford, "did you, son?"

"Gosh, no," he said. "How many kids can say their dad won a solid gold football?"

"It may not really be *solid* gold, Mike," said Buford, touched by the adulation. "But I admit I'm mighty proud of it."

Mike, in looking up to his father, caught sight for a second time of the gun rack across the room. "Were all those yours?" he asked.

Buford sighed, as he studied the clean display of rifles and shotguns. He went to the rack and hefted a particular shotgun. After checking it, he gazed out the window. "My grandpa gave me this gun when I was nine years old."

Mike's eyes widened with the anticipation of possession, and for a second it seemed as though the gun would be his. But a sound interrupted the possible ceremony. Pauline and Dwana had entered the room. Buford looked to the door in

15

time to see the stricken expression in his wife's eyes. He pulled the gun back and replaced it on its pegs.

"And when you're nine, Mike," said Buford, "we might just talk about it."

Mike, deeply disappointed, looked at his mother and then back to his dad. "Gee. I'm *almost* nine."

Pauline had created the crisis, and she was quick to assume control. "Grandma's making cookies downstairs," she announced.

Since cookies were something he could have right away, Mike was easily bought off. "I get the bowl!" he said, already on the run.

"I get the spoon!" said Dwana on his heels.

After a stiff pause, Pauline relaxed. "Thank you," she said.

Buford shrugged it off. "Nothing wrong with guns," he said, drawing Pauline close to him. "In the right hands."

Chapter Two

Peace, a Good Home ... and a Future

Buford couldn't recall how diligently he might have served his father in those days long ago, but he was attacking the chores with vigor on this occasion. He wanted to work hard, awaken new muscles, and feel the hard-earned sweat of toil. All he had to do was recall the sweat he had expended worthlessly during those millennium years as a wrestler. The memory was enough to drive him to frenetic zeal.

"Hey, slow down there, son," said his father, as Buford tossed a coil of logging chain into the flatbed truck. "I thought athletes learned how to pace themselves."

Buford laughed breathlessly, and took out a borrowed kerchief to mop his brow. He was shirtless, and the bulging muscles of his torso gleamed like a damp statue in a Greek courtyard. "This is play, dad ... real play. I like to play hard."

During his break, Buford let his gaze sweep the panorama of green, wooded hills surrounding the farm.

Grandpa watched him for a moment, and nodded with full understanding. "Wonderin' why you ever left this place, Buford?"

"You guessed it," he said, drawing in a breath of fresh country air.

Grandpa, who stood close to six feet, had to reach above his head to place a friendly hand on his son's shoulder. "We all make mistakes," Grandpa said in the philosophical tone Buford

17

remembered so well, "but the smart man don't make the same one twice. Now you take Parker Forsythe—his place has three hundred acres—he never learned that gasoline and white lightin' just don't mix—'til God reminded him one night where State Highway meets Route Seven." Buford was silent in a contemplative pause. His father had a way of telegraphing important messages, and this would be one. "So, his allotted piece of earth is back on the market. Only six thousand down, furnished. Has a right nice house, and three new catfish ponds. The estate has a timber lease, too." Another long pause. "Now if a man had a partner . . . with some loggin' gear. . . ."

Buford grinned and faced his father directly. "Tell me something, dad? When did you tell the bank we'd look at it?"

After all the subtlety of the buildup, Buford soon discovered that the appointment had been made for late the next morning. The entire family turned out for the inspection. Even before he had his first glimpse of the place, Buford knew he would be visiting his new home. If it hadn't been just right for them, his father would never have brought it up.

In truth, the property was much more than Buford could conjure in his mind. The trim, green-shuttered cottage sat snugly on a small knoll surrounded by towering oaks. At the base of the knoll were the three catfish ponds, in a setting of scrub pines and reeds. Birds and wildlife were visibly abundant, even from the distant vantage point.

The children and Shep turned their first interest to the fish ponds. Grandpa dipped a pail of fish food from a handy bin, and scattered a handful over the water. The water came alive in response, with hundreds of fish leaping and thrashing for nourishment. Dozens of them broke the surface of the pond. This was a great adventure for Shep, who had never seen a fish in action. He barked excitedly while the children took turns with the feeding.

After the tour of the house, Buford and Pauline stood alone next to a tire swing that had been suspended from the high branch of a backyard tree. Buford took his wife into his arms. "It's perfect, isn't it?" he whispered into her ear. She nodded, nestling closer. "I have a good feeling about it, Pauline. We had each other before, but now we'll have everything, peace, a good home . . . a future."

"I'm so happy, honey . . . I could almost. . . ."

"Hey . . . none of that," he said, when tears welled in her eyes. "We left all the tears way behind."

With a sniffle, Pauline smiled and straightened. "The first thing we do is to sell the trailer . . . so we won't ever be tempted to. . . ."

Buford laughed aloud. "I knew you'd say that." He reached into his shirt pocket and served her a check with a flourish. "Sold it this morning, early."

"For *me*?" she said, clutching it.

"For us," Buford replied.

"Oh, Buford," she said, having to turn her head. "Now I know I'm going to cry."

Just in case somebody had a sudden change of heart, the Pussers made a speedy trip to the Bank of Selmer. The down payment was made and all the papers were prepared on the spot.

After the hours of negotiation, all three generations of Pussers gathered in front of the modern bank building. Across the street in the center of the town square sat the County Courthouse, its benches overflowing with townfolk and country visitors. The bank was the most modern building in town, but the courthouse was most imposing, with its four colonial columns and red brick construction.

"Here it is," Buford said to Pauline. "The deed and mortgage to your first real home. Happy?"

After securing the papers in her purse, she managed to kiss Buford's cheek, unable to voice her planned reply. The racket of a fast-charging pickup truck diverted her attention. With all eyes alerted to possible disaster the truck screeched to a stop mid-lane across the street. A beaming round face was craning out of the cab window.

"Buford! Buford!" shouted the wild man in the red-checked shirt and straw hat with cowboy blocking. "It's me . . . Lutie!"

Before Buford could respond, the pickup burned rubber in a leaping surge forward. It took a wild squealing arch, made a rocking U-turn that didn't quite work out. To compensate for the limited steering ratio, the truck bounded into a gas station ramp and out the other side. It came to a screeching halt a few yards from the Pusser gathering.

"That," said Buford, grinning, "is Lutie McVeigh. He played end on our football team." Buford shook his head. "Crazy Lutie . . . he dropped more passes than he ever caught . . . but was always good for a laugh."

An understanding wife, Pauline said, "Grandma and I have lots of shopping to do, and you'd just be in the way. Take your time, dear. I'll go home with her."

Lutie had moved ahead to angle his pickup into a parking space, waving frantically as he did it. "Are you sure?" Buford asked Pauline.

"Positive," she said, with another kiss. "Come on, Grandma."

Grandma lingered just a moment. Her eyes were saying more than her words. "One thing, Buford," she said with a hand on his arm. "If you look around town, you might see some changes. But pay them no mind. They've got nothin' to do with us."

As Buford attempted to decipher her cryptic message, Lutie was upon him, slapping his shoulder, feinting a left to the stomach. In the height of the greeting, the departing Pussers moved off toward the shops.

"I heard it, but I didn't believe it!" Lutie fired away, in stuttering gasps of excitement. "The old Forsythe place, I just heard. Buford Pusser, they said. Must be *another* Buford Pusser, I said. Ain't nobody gonna tame that wild bull *I* knew. Not down to no dirt farmin' and catfish feedin'!"

"Good to see you, Lutie," Buford said, finally.

"Why a man'd have to be crazy to give up those faraway places with strange soundin' dames!" After a pause to laugh at his own joke, Lutie asked: "You *didn't?*"

" 'Fraid I did. I've come home to roost."

Lutie nodded toward the departing Pauline. "The old lady—and a pretty one she is—kinda leaned on you, huh? Settle down, grow roots,

21

or Daddy ain't gonna have any more *fun*, she said? Come on, it's old Lutie . . . you can level with me."

Buford laughed. "Nothing like that. I just got tired of being a trained animal in somebody else's circus is all. Uh, how about a beer?"

"Only refused a beer once," he said, digging an elbow into Buford's ribs, " 'n that was offered over the telephone."

Lutie grabbed Buford's arm and began leading him. His banter and laughter gave little room for Buford to comment. "Emmie Dayton's got seven kids now . . . two by her own husband," he said, grinning to the point where his dimples were turning red from use. "And, oh . . . Grady Coker's a deputy sheriff . . . case you need a ticket fixed. . . ."

"Lutie," Buford cut in. "Where are we heading . . . Chuck and Babe's?"

"Oh man, you're really outa touch. That place is a museum now . . . strictly for senior citizens. Why they're playin' *checkers* on the bar. We're big city, Buford. We got our own sin, gamblin', crime, vice . . . and twenty-four hours a day. A man like you will feel right at home."

Buford didn't really believe the wild claims, recalling Lutie's tendency to exaggerate. He began to believe, however, after driving the station wagon a few miles under Lutie's frantic direction. They drew to a stop in front of a modernistic bar called the Green Lantern.

Buford couldn't believe what he was seeing. In the moments they were parked across the street, Buford saw a pair of sexily dressed girls leading two men toward a group of nearby house trailers. The men, obviously drunk, were separated by the girls, who took them inside different trailers.

"How about this, huh?" Lutie said. "A shopping center for sinners! You can lay a bet, a broad, or go on a three-day drunk. Brought more business to this town than anything since the cotton gin."

At Lutie's further direction, Buford turned a corner down the main road until they arrived at a beer tavern called Lucky Spot. Much the same situation was evident there. This was apparently Lutie's destination, because he was already out of the car. As they walked toward the door, under a bright red and yellow sign, a girl, very young, in scant shorts and revealing sweater clung to a drunk's arm until he was shut inside one of the convenient trailers.

In a way, Buford was glad for Lutie's loquacity. With his perpetual banter, Buford could postpone a definite reaction. At this moment, he was simply stunned.

"An oasis for the weary traveler," Lutie continued. "Home for the wicked. Soothin' balm for the frustrated husband." He poked an elbow once more in Buford's ribs. "You know ... some gals even give tradin' stamps to keep the old lady from wakin' up the kids when you come home. Sodom an' Gomorrah. . . . Here comes Buford the Bull ... no holds barred!"

Buford, with considerable reluctance, followed Lutie through the front doors of the Lucky Spot. A strange foreboding told him this stop would not be very lucky at all. Still, he followed.

Chapter Three

Leaving the hot, Tennessee sunshine behind, they plunged into a pit of blasting sound and darkness. The jukebox reverberated the full decibel rendition of a country and western tune, as Buford followed Lutie toward the long bar that ran the length of the far wall. When his eyes adjusted, Buford could see that midday business was good at the Lucky Spot. In the rays of revolving colored lights, several couples could be seen scattered in booths, and another four or five couples sat crouched over the bar. The decor was western, but the numerous girls that inhabited the place were out of costume. No fringed culottes and tasseled sombreros for them. The girls on the day shift at the Lucky Spot wore as little clothing as possible.

Buford's eyes swept the first girl at the end of the bar. She wore a low-cut halter and skin-tight slacks. She looked about nineteen. In the cluster of expectant bar girls, there was a wide range in age and image. Some were almost cherubic in their youth; others showed age and hard mileage.

"Gonna break training, gents?" said the pug-bartender.

"Lightly," said Buford, taking one of the vacant stools. "Two beers."

As Buford pulled out his roll and peeled off a twenty, two of the watchful young women stirred from their stools to move toward the center of the bar. By the time the cans of beer were delivered, the female welcoming committee had also arrived.

"Hiya, Lutie," said the small girl with very large breasts. She spoke to Lutie but wasn't watching him. Her eyes were for Buford.

"Why if it ain't li'l ole Margie Ann," Lutie said, drawing her close to him. "I haven't seen you in hours."

She accepted the mauling, but her attention didn't stray. "And who may this be?" she said. "Superman . . . Tarzan . . . King Kong?"

"This is my bodyguard . . . Buford," Lutie said, as Margie Ann's finger traced a line over the bulging muscles of Buford's arm.

"There's enough man here for *three* of us," she said.

"Only if he gets the group rate, darlin'," said Lutie, turning to the bartender who had returned with Buford's change. "These gals are tinder dry, Bozo. . . . Wet 'em down."

Buford sipped at his beer, ignoring the attention he was getting. As the girls sat on either side of Lutie, Buford gazed to the end of the bar. A girl was paying for a bottle, which she then carried with her to a corner booth where two men and another girl waited. On his reverse scan of the room, Buford's eyes lingered over a very attractive girl who appeared in an inner doorway. She was young, perhaps in her early twenties, and wore tight black slacks. If Buford's eyesight was as good as he thought it was, that was just about *all* the girl was wearing. He looked back to his beer as she started toward him.

Buford had no doubts where the girl would sit, and despite his resolutions otherwise, Buford found his eyes glancing to the stool beside him. No, his eyesight hadn't deteriorated. The girl wore a blouse that was totally see-through. A pair of firm round breasts with pink nipples seemed to stare at him mockingly. He turned away quickly.

"Ha, Ho!" Lutie wailed in delight at Buford's embarrassment. "You gotta git used to them kinda things. You ain't seen nothin' yet, Buford."

"Beer," said the girl, crossing her legs.

"On me," Lutie said immediately.

During a sip of beer, Buford couldn't resist another sidelong glance at the adjacent spectacle.

"Looking," she said blowing smoke in Buford's face, "is free."

"Down, Luan," Lutie warned pleasantly. "You girls just drink your pacifiers . . . I'll tell you when."

Luan started to speak to Buford, but Lutie cut her off. "Now . . . the next stop on our little tour." He crammed his change into his pocket, grabbed his beer, and stood up from his stool. "Come on bodyguard, I'll show you some real action."

As he was dragged off, Buford managed a final peek at the firm young breasts. The girl was smiling confidently. "Take it easy, Lutie," Buford said. "What's the rush."

"We gotta pay for all this action, ain't we?" Lutie said leading Buford to the draped doorway from where Luan had emerged earlier. "Stick with me, I'll show you how."

They entered a square cement-block room that was alive with activity. In a corner there were two poker tables with all seats occupied, and in the center of the room was a crap table lined with anxious players. The gamblers ranged from men wearing conservative business suits to farmers in overalls. There were a stickman and two crap dealers operating the game. A bouncer was also evident as he walked between tables collecting poker chips. One wall was lined with slot machines, all of which were operating, and interspersed among the dozens of customers were the everpresent hustlers.

Buford took it all in, but couldn't really believe it. Wide open gambling in McNairy County? Incredible. As Lutie led the way through the crowd, Buford took note of the steel-caged cashier's window. A mild-appearing man with white hair was counting a stack of money that would soon be deposited in the huge steel safe behind him. There was nothing temporary about this setup. The operators were obviously sure of themselves.

Lutie lost no time in elbowing up to the dice table. He bought a stack of chips and placed two of them in front of him. The dice thrower, wearing hard hat and work clothes, blew into his cupped hands ready to deliver.

"The point is six," the stickman sang out.

"And six it is!" warned the hard-hat as he threw.

"Seven . . . a loser," The stickman announced. "Make your come bets. Coming out again."

Buford watched for a few more throws, but lost interest. He strolled around the room sipping his beer, with his thoughts far removed from the strange scene he was part of. He was speculating over his recently acquired home, and how good things would be now that he was aimed in the right direction. He watched a farmer lose what must have been a week's earnings at the quarter slot machine, and was relieved when he saw Lutie coming toward him through the crowd. He had been ready to leave five minutes after he arrived.

"Had enough, have you?" Buford asked amiably.

"I know I can get 'em," Lutie said, smacking his fist into his palm. "Lady luck just sent me a smile. Better let me have fifty, Buford . . . just 'til we get back to town."

Buford hadn't expected this, and didn't particularly care for the idea of financing Lutie's gambling binge. He frowned momentarily, but let it trail into a sigh. He took out his roll, and when fifty was counted out, Lutie grabbed it without ceremony or thanks. He rushed back to the table. Now, with his own money invested, Buford was more interested. He moved to the dice table after Lutie.

Buford couldn't believe the losing streak Lutie was running, but knowing him he wasn't surprised. Even back in the football days there had been a certain McVeigh predilection for doom. Lutie was simply running true to form. Then, something seemed to alert Buford. From that point forward he watched with increasing scrutiny.

"Seven . . . a loser," said the stickman, "but it's always darkest before the dawn."

Buford chose a new vantage point. He took station behind a cute and sexy blonde wearing a backless halter. He wasn't interested in the blonde, but he *was* interested in the shooter who stood beside her. From where he stood, he could look over her head with an unimpeded view.

"Lay your bets, gentlemen," the stickman said in his special monotone. "Lady luck is spreading her legs." After the bets were placed: "The point is ten. Ten's the point. Hard way open."

Now Buford watched with keen interest. The stickman tossed the dice back to the burly shooter. He scooped them up, blew on them, gave them a rattle, and started to throw. In a move fast enough to catch an airborne fly, Buford reached over the blonde and grabbed the hand mid-air. He rapped the wrist against the edge of the table. The hand popped open and four dice tumbled onto the green-topped table. All eyes turned to Buford . . . silence.

"The point is seventeen," Buford said coldly.

The stickman broke the nervous silence. "You're not rolling, wise guy."

Buford drew in a breath, ready. "My money is."

The dice thrower edged out of range, and the other players began to back away. Buford and Lutie remained where they were. Buford felt bodies moving in on him, and was about to move across the room to the wall. Lutie's sudden anger detoured him.

"Why you dirty bastards!" Lutie shouted in delayed realization of what had been happening. "You stacked the damn dice on me!"

The bouncer, who had been perched center room on a high stool, was the man behind Buford now. He eased his right hand into brass knuckles, and with a vicious arch of his arm,

29

brought the metal-laden fist down on Buford's head. Buford sprawled forward, face down against the table. In reflex, Lutie leaped on the back of the bouncer. By this time the stickman and two poker dealers were moving in, but Buford was ready.

He assessed the situation in a glance, and decided Lutie was in the most immediate danger. The bouncer wrestled Lutie to the floor and was about to drive the brass knucks into his face. Buford halted that action with a swift but accurate left fist to the jaw. The bouncer's body flew into the path of the approaching dealers.

Buford turned to his right to see the stickman standing on the dice table. His foot was already on its way to his head. Buford lurched back just enough. When the toe passed his chin, he grabbed the ankle, and with a fierce twisting movement, slammed the stickman to the floor. He was about to follow him down, but one of the dealers was upon him. Buford dispatched him with a elbow to the groin, but another was there. Buford gave the second dealer a knee-lift that carried him a foot into the air. Buford began to feel he was in command. He moved unsmiling, catlike, anticipating all possibilities.

Twice the bouncer came back, and Buford met him each time. Once a fist to the mouth slammed him against a poker table, smashing it to splinters. The second time, Buford put him away with a double fist to the throat. But by this time the outside bar had been alerted and the odds were diminishing. Buford took several jolts to the head, but managed to drive a fist into the face of the stickman. This was one more who would be out of the melee. He felt his fist tear the jaw from its hinges.

When he lurched out of the bartender's grasp, Buford lifted his knee to the crotch. When Bozo bent over, Buford brought a double fist upward that seemed to snap his head from his shoulders. Another man, a new face, came toward Buford with a chair, but he wasn't fast enough. Buford sidestepped, grabbed him by the crotch and throat, and threw him across the room.

Buford looked around in time to see one of the recent bar arrivals finish Lutie with a vicious fist into the mouth. Lutie gasped, blood streaming out of his mouth. His jaw was shattered. Buford grabbed Lutie's attacker, flipped him upside down, and slammed his head into the floor. When he sprawled, Buford kicked him in the throat.

Buford was immediately in a struggle with three men. He used fists, knees, and shoulders to free himself. He elbowed one of them, forearmed another, and drop-kicked the third.

Buford had crossed out the bouncer, but he shouldn't have. He was back, with a roll of quarters in his fist. He connected to Buford's jaw, slamming him against the dice table. But not for long. Buford bounced back at him, caught hold, and lifted him over his head. He drove his body against the far wall and followed him there. He threw a shoulder into his solar plexus and clubbed him with his right fist when he bounced off the wall. The bouncer slumped to his knees, blood streaming from his eyes, nose, and sagging mouth.

Buford felt the battle was over, and it was.

But he hadn't won. Someone had brought a whiskey bottle from the bar. He slammed it over Buford's head. When Buford pitched to the floor, three men began to go to work with brass knuckles. Another moved in to slam him across the face with a 38 caliber revolver. There was little strength left in Buford, but the three men still had all they could handle. When they had him pinned on the dice table, the bouncer crawled to his feet. Holding his drooping jaw, he moved to the center of the room.

"Okay . . . let's teach this punk who runs things around here!" he said. "Take care of him, Otie."

Buford was pinned and had nothing left but his consciousness. He watched with sick fascination as the man named Otie whipped out a long switchblade knife. He leaned over and slashed the blade across Buford's chest. Buford let out a scream that cleared the bar girls who had been watching from the door. Again and again the blade dug into Buford's flesh. After the third deep-burning slash, Buford was blessed with unconsciousness.

Chapter Four

"I'll Die If I Don't Get Help."

It was a dream, wasn't it? His mother looked so young. But as the dream progressed he was vaguely aware it was more than that. It was reality too; a true dream. His mother was there before him, but so was he. The boy standing at the door with the pout on his face was himself. It was as though he were watching a home movie that kept fading in and out of focus.

"But I don't want to go to school, Ma. They don't like me. I want to stay here with you."

"Buford . . . if your father hears you talk like that, he'll skin you alive. He always says I'm not strict enough . . . and maybe he's right."

Buford didn't want to make trouble for his mother. He nodded sadly, took a deep breath, and left the house through the kitchen door. He would catch the school bus as ordered, but he wouldn't like it. He just didn't get along at school. The girls teased him, and all the boys made fun of him. They expected him to laugh and yell and play their stupid games, but he couldn't do it. It was as if he were being tied up inside. He couldn't make friends, and unless threatened with severe punishment wouldn't even sound his voice in class. And this was only the third grade. To think of nine more years of such torture was beyond imagination.

The face of his mother faded from view. As she drifted away, Buford managed to call after her. "I'm sorry, Ma. I'm sorry I hurt your feelings."

As he moaned after the departing figure, a new scene came before him, and Buford was startled. It was crazy. What kind of a dream was this? It was too real; too painful. He was viewing another good-bye, but age had begun to show in his mother's face, and this image of Buford found him tall and very thin. He remembered this day. He had quit school after a few weeks into the tenth grade. He had that pipeline job in Oklahoma, and he was reassuring his mother that everything would work out. He would work hard and give her all the things she wanted in life.

Before he could follow the events that brought him back to high school, and after graduation into the Marine Corps, a strange calling sound echoed into his consciousness. It wasn't a voice he recognized, but it had a friendly quality. It was calling him back. "No . . . can't. Too much pain."

He forcibly drew himself back into this curious world of dreams. He arrived into his fantasy with a medical discharge clutched in his hand. He wore the uniform still, but it no longer belonged.

"I don't have asthma. I'm strong as an ox."

But the Marine Corps thought otherwise, and once more he was rejected. This time he was coming home, and the occasion wasn't a happy one. He had failed, after only a few months as a Marine.

Before he could relive the embarrassment of the explanations at home, he skipped ahead a few days. He and his pals went to Memphis—

34

didn't they?—to visit his sister, Gailye. It was a good reunion and everything was fine. Buford groaned when his mind progressed to the trip home. It was after midnight, and it was raining, and the lights of an oncoming car flashed into his consciousness. Billy Earl Christopher was driving, Buford recalled, and if he hadn't left the road the collision would have been far worse. He remembered lying in a ravine with the rain pelting him. He couldn't move for the excruciating pain in his back. He remembered, too, the voices discussing him during the ambulance race to Baptist Hospital in Memphis. They were saying how miraculous it was that anyone had survived the wreck, and that they thought Buford had a broken back.

This confused him. That was years ago; a few days before his nineteenth birthday in 1956. Was he reliving it *exactly?* He heard his own voice as it moaned with pain, and now—not in a dream —it was raining. He was sure of it, and he also had the feeling he was lying along the road somewhere . . . but where?

The sound of a semitrailer-truck broke through. He opened his eyes to see the beam of bright headlights darting through the overhead branches. It screamed past, returning his cloak of darkness. The rain fell harder, and he moved his head aside to keep the deluge out of his eyes. "Oh, God," he moaned aloud. "Am I dying? Won't I see them again . . . Pauline. . . ."

Another car zipped past, and in the moment of light he managed to lift his head and look down at his chest. His shirt was torn, matted with thick blood. In the gathering pool beside him, the water was red. He tried to rise, but the pain sent him back to obscurity.

He didn't know how long he was unconscious this time, but he knew he had been unconscious. He also knew this was not November 26, 1956. It was now, today, and fragments of recent memory began to feed back to him. Then anger erupted, and despite pain that was impossible to bear, he managed to get to his hands and knees to crawl.

It was an interminable climb, a rock at a time, a clump of weeds. He would advance up the muddy bank a foot and slide back three, but somehow, sometime, he reached the roadside. He lay next to the road and watched the headlights beaming toward him. He would lift an arm and try to call out, but with the rain and darkness he couldn't be seen.

"Damn!" he cried out, fighting the pain that had risen from numbness. "I'll die if I don't get help."

He crawled to the very edge of the macadam road inch by inch. When a car came bearing down on him, he managed to raise his body to wave. The brakes squealed and the car stopped. "Oh, thank God . . . thank you, God!"

But with a shifting of gears, the car curved around him and sped off down the rain-swept highway. Several other cars passed him, splattering mud in his face; others slowed and drove on. Buford sobbed in frustration and anger. Somehow he got to his knees and crawled into the center of the lane. He held his hands in prayer, with his eyes cast upward. The next car would stop. It would stop or it would kill him. "However you will it, God!" he cried to the heavens.

He heard a truck before it reached the rise in the road, and then he could feel the illumination of the headlights as the speeding vehicle bore down on him. He didn't look; he prayed. He heard air brakes squish, and tires squeal. Then silence. Two men ran to him from the cab. His prayers had been answered.

Time lost all meaning to Buford. His mind filled with fragments of thoughts, some real, some imagined. He recalled his refusal of hospital treatment. He had to get to his home where Pauline would be waiting, where his roots were now planted. The truck drivers argued the point, but Buford won out. They drove him several miles out of their way to deliver him to the cottage on the knoll above the catfish ponds. Buford questioned his own judgment, however, when Pauline opened the door to meet him. With her cry of alarm, all memory stopped —at least for the moment.

He was fully conscious as Dr. Stivers worked over him, and he was intermittently aware of the voices in the next room. . . . They were all there by now. It was morning and there was sunlight after the storm. The storm was over and he was still alive. He was alive, and his family had gathered outside to await the doctor's report. Buford tried desperately to put together the pieces of the nightmare that preceded his unconsciousness, but the events returned only in patches. Somehow he felt guilty for what had happened. The guilt was felt, however, for those close to him. He regretted the anguish he had brought them. But as the doctor cleansed and sutured, Buford's emotions began to alter. Soon, he had room for nothing but revenge.

Sheriff Al Thurman had already tried to speak to Buford, but he couldn't bring up enough strength to repeat the details he had already told Pauline. But the sheriff was still outside in the living room, as was his deputy, Grady Coker. He could hear their voices along with Pauline's and his mother's and father's.

Buford saw the wrinkled face of the doctor relax with a sigh. "That should do it, Buford." he said, beginning to put away his instruments. "Too bad I had to make this kind of visit after so many years."

"Glad—you could make it, Doc."

"You'll be getting sleepy soon," said the doctor, snapping his black satchel, and running a hand through his white hair. "Gave you a sedative. Pauline's got some pain pills for later on. You'll be needing them."

"No," said Buford, sleepily. "I won't need them."

The doctor paused at the side of the bed. "Don't be too sure. I haven't seen many men take what you took."

"I have to feel the pain, Doc . . . have to remember."

The doctor managed a firm smile, and gave Buford's arm a pat. "I'll drop back tonight. Try to rest easy, son."

Buford nodded, and lay back in the bed. How ironic it was. He had just spent his first night in his new home, and under what kind of circumstances? So this was the new life. At the moment it didn't seem very much better than the old one, did it? Buford was drowsy, but kept awake when the words in the next room began to penetrate his consciousness.

"You should have called a seamstress," he heard Doc say. "Took some two hundred stitches in him."

Then Pauline's voice: "Five years in the ring and he has to come home to get half killed."

"Ordinary man wouldn't have made it through," the doc said. "Where can I wash up?"

Buford heard Sheriff Thurman ask Pauline where it happened. When she told him, Thurman said: "Obvious he got liquored up . . . dead drunk, right, Doc?"

"That isn't obvious at all," the doctor answered. "Important thing to you should be who did it to him."

"Yes, Thurman." It was Buford's father speaking. "And who threw him down a ravine to die . . . and where's his station wagon?"

Buford agonized, listening to his father upset himself in the growing argument with the sheriff. He charged the sheriff with dereliction, and the sheriff defended his position by saying men have to let off steam and he only tried to keep it in bounds. Then Buford's father threatened that the voters might just want a change come election time.

"Not like you to threaten a man, Carl," said the sheriff in rising anger.

Then the doctor spoke up. "He speaks for more than himself."

Then a voice trailed in that Buford hadn't expected. It was little Mike. "If my daddy was sheriff nobody would be mean to anybody."

Buford's eyes clouded with tears. That was his family speaking up for him . . . his wonderful family. He drifted into troubled sleep.

The doctor was right about the pain, but Buford refused to take the pills Pauline held for him. Every ache and sting and spasm was important to him; something he chose to suffer and file away in his mind. Then, when the time came, he would have no trouble recalling it— all of it—all of every detail of the debt he would one day repay.

The storm clouds hung over McNairy County for several days as though to provide an appropriate backdrop for Buford's festering rage. Finally the sun returned, and Buford accepted Pauline's invitation to sit on the patio. She had bought a metal table with umbrella and new patio furniture. Buford nodded his approval, and rather enjoyed the sunshine for a change. He spent hours honing a fine edge to his new ax. He tested the edge with his thumb, frowned and began the circular motion once more against the wet stone he brought with him.

A short time later, Pauline came from the house with a pitcher of iced tea. Buford watched her, forcing a smile as she approached. When she stepped to the wooden deck where he sat, he started to speak to her. He realized how withdrawn he had been, and knew it was unfair to burden his family with his personal grudge. Before he could speak, they were both diverted by the sound of an approaching car.

Any inclination toward conviviality was halted now. His expression hardened as the sheriff's car came to a stop in the driveway below. He watched solemnly as Al Thurman and Grady Coker got out of the car and climbed the rolling lawn toward where he sat. This was the first real look he had had of his former teammate, Grady, in several years. He looked rather fit, Buford thought. But Thurman was another matter. He was fat now, and red faced. The good life had taken its toll. It was human nature for Buford to size every man for action. It was a residual from his ring career.

Grady spoke first. "Feeling better, Buford?"

He nodded as he tested the ax blade. "Guess so, Grady . . . physically at least."

Thurman pushed his Stetson back in apparent frustration. "Can't find tire, nor bolt of your station wagon anywhere, Buford." he said with a sigh. "Neither can the State Police."

"So, it just vanished," said Buford.

"Happens all the time," Thurman said. "Professionals, most likely. They repaint, file the numbers . . . you know. And . . . as for the fracas at the Lucky Spot . . . can't find a single witness that saw it your way."

"There's always Lutie," Buford said.

"Now, Buford," Thurman said gesturing. "You know Lutie . . . crazy Lutie McVeigh? Can't ever tell where the truth ends with him and the B.S. begins. There ain't a soul in McNairy County who takes him serious."

"I do."

"Well . . . if that's your whole case, you ain't got one."

Buford felt his neck get warm. "I got a chest full of stitches."

"Well, if that's all," said Thurman taking off his hat and examining the sweat band,

41

"then count your blessings . . . and drop the case."

In a move of raging spontaneity, Buford swung the ax into the boards between Thurman's feet. The sheriff's hand instinctively reached for his nickle-plated magnum, but halted just short of drawing it. Pauline, in fearful reaction, clutched Buford's shoulder.

"I'm dropping nothing!" Buford said in white fury. His eyes met Thurman's as he stepped back and dropped his shaking hand from his weapon.

"Then . . . it's your funeral," Thurman said coldly. He glared at Buford a moment and started toward his cruiser.

"I've known you since I was a kid, Thurman," Buford called after him. "I always thought you walked *tall!* Looks to me like you've learned to crawl!"

Pauline kneaded Buford's shoulder. "Please, Buford . . . remember your stitches. . . ."

"How could I forget them?" Buford answered. He looked up sharply at Grady who remained behind. "What about *you*, Grady? You going to let them throw me in a hole and cover me up?"

Grady leaned forward so as not to be heard by Thurman. "What can *I* do, Buford? He deals the cards . . . I can only play the hand I get."

"Then you better find yourself a new game."

Thurman turned back and shouted, "Coker! Get down here . . . *fast!*"

With a shrug of helplessness, Grady hurried after his boss. Pauline continued to cling to Buford's shoulder as the sheriff and his deputy got into the car and slammed the doors. Thurman revved the engine wildly, and spun the car around in a slag spitting departure.

"There it is again," Buford said icily.

"What, honey?" Pauline asked.

"The system. Live *my* way . . . or don't live at all!"

Pauline didn't speak. She kissed Buford's cheek, and poured him a glass of cool tea. Buford stared down the road unaware that the birds had begun to sing again. There was serenity in his little home on a hill in southwestern Tennessee, but Buford wasn't ready just now to accept it.

Chapter Five

"You Have To Seek Your Own Justice Here."

The doctor warned him and Pauline begged him, but nothing was going to keep Buford an invalid when his body told him otherwise. Within no more than ten days after the incident at the Lucky Spot, Buford was working hand in hand with his father. His father knew there would be no curbing his stubborn son's will, so he reluctantly agreed to begin the logging operation. Buford was aware of his father's personal pain when his stitches broke open, and he wished it could be otherwise. But he had to work and work hard. He needed every grain of strength he could muster; it was important that he return to fighting weight and top condition.

Every time Doc Stivers patched him up, he issued a lecture, and Buford was courteously responsive. The man was doing his job so he listened, but the words held no meaning. Doctor or not . . . no man can dictate the capability of another man's body. If Buford hadn't been sure of what he was doing, he wouldn't have been doing it. He was driven and his instincts were seldom wrong.

A portable saw mill was being staged deep into Buford's property. As several hired hands were busily cleaning brush, Buford and his father directed the release of a load of logs from one of the two trucks at the site. The chain that cinched them was unfastened, and the men used logging picks to roll the heavy timber to the ground. Buford, wearing Levi's and a T-shirt, lifted a huge rotary saw blade and fitted it onto its shaft. As he bolted it together, a dilapidated logging truck emerged from the woods and entered the clearing. A tall and husky black man jumped down from the cab and placed a rock behind one of the wheels. Buford squinted in recognition.

"Just like clockwork," said Buford's father. "Every time we start a new operation, here comes that damn boy and his beat-up truck . . . lookin' for a job."

Buford looked at his father in disbelief, but didn't remark. Instead he jumped from the mill platform and strode toward the truck. When Buford neared the other man, they both stopped and stared.

"Buford!" the black man exclaimed.

"Obra Eaker!" Buford greeted. He went to the man and gave him an arm-slapping handshake. "Hey . . . you've really filled out, man . . . you and I could make one heck of a tag team."

Obra laughed. "Maybe we still can."

As they spoke, Obra looked toward Buford's father who stood watching them with folded arms. The glance brought Obra up straight. "Uh . . . you wouldn't happen to have a job, would you? For a man and his truck?" Obra asked diffidently. "I'm used to hard work and low pay."

"Got a loader?" Buford asked.

"Can get one in a hurry."

"Good. We need help . . . and the pay is the same for everyone. I'll go tell the boss."

45

"Thanks, Buford," Obra said, shaking his hand vigorously. "Thanks . . . a lot."

Buford joined his father as the old truck started up and began to weave its way over the makeshift logging road toward the highway. "Pa," Buford said, "you got something against Obra? We could sure use another good hand."

"Why I've known him since he was a pickaninny . . . hired his pa many times."

"That doesn't tell me anything."

"Well," said his father, sheepishly, "he got himself educated an' all, and came down with a ragin' case of that new social disease . . . Black Power."

Buford grinned. "Is *that* all?"

"Now, don't you get me wrong," his father qualified. "I believe in equality. I just don't like it forced on me."

"It's going to be a lot of fun," said Buford, "working with the two of you." Buford left his father, who was scratching his head in puzzlement. He started the gasoline engine that powered the saw.

A day later the mill was in full operation. Buford ran a log through the saw, and was about to feed it another when he saw Obra releasing timber from his battered truck. He stopped what he was doing to help out. One log hadn't cleared the truck bed, so Buford hoisted himself up and took hold of one end. Obra struggled with the other.

"Hey, wait a minute, man," said Obra, grunting. "Give me a chance."

Buford laughed as the log fell clear. He wiped his forehead and glanced at the noonday sun. "Looks like lunch time to me," he said. He jumped from the truck. "How about it, Obie?"

Obra complied with a thumbs up signal, and reached into the truck cab for his lunch bag. Buford went to the saw crew to tell them to shut down, and picked up his own lunch bucket. He joined Obra on a shaded log pile, and each man ate his lunch in silence. Halfway through his second huge sandwich, Buford gave up. He put the uneaten portion into his bucket, and reached over for a long oak-bough that had been roughly scaled to the size of a giant baseball bat. He began to shave at it with his knife.

Obra continued gnawing on a sandwich, but was more interested in what Buford was doing. "You planning to play Teddy Roosevelt, Buford?"

"Hm?"

"I mean . . . are you planning to 'walk softly and carry a big stick' or something?"

"I've been thinking about it," Buford said, taking an angry chunk out of the wood, "when I get well enough."

Obra grinned. "How does it feel . . . being part of the oppressed minority?"

"You ought to know," Buford said, managing a smile of his own. "Any suggestions?"

"First . . . never beat your head against a wall," he said holding up one finger. "It might fall on you. Two . . ." Two fingers were raised. "Lone wolves are easy prey. You've got to organize. And three." This time he emphasized the three fingers in front of Buford's face. "You're a damn fool for trying what I know you're going to do." The old friends stared at each other in mutual understanding.

47

Doc Stiver described it as a miracle: the way Buford recovered. But Buford knew better. It was no miracle, but will had a lot to do with it. Ever since those miserable early days of school, Buford set out to make himself someone special. Once he overcame his built-in doubts and fears, he dedicated his life toward becoming a bit tougher, stronger—and if necessary—meaner than the next man. Not that he wanted to hurt anyone unnecessarily, but when a man is as good as he can get, he is less vulnerable, less likely to get stepped on. Buford took a lot of sand in the face as a youngster, but never again. He just couldn't take being pushed around.

As for his healing ability, it was much the same. He couldn't stand to have anyone nurse him, look after him. He figured any accident he might have was his own doing. It might not have been his fault, but he got himself into it. So why should someone outside himself suffer the consequences.

Buford healed readily after that bad wreck in November 1956. The doctors said he'd probably be a cripple the rest of his life. He was walking tall again within two months. Then, there was that other ugly episode down in Mississippi, only a couple months later. He got into a dice game and had a streak of good luck. He was sure he would run his final seventy-five dollars of Marine pay into a small fortune. But they wouldn't let him quit when he was ahead. There was a fight, and Buford ended up in an alley, beaten, robbed, and stabbed. From that day forward he hated gambling games and gambling places. He supposed he carried the shoulder chip into the Lucky Spot that afternoon with Lutie. So, he got into it, didn't he? Once again it was true, and once again he would mend his wounds and seek his own justice. It was his way of life.

Without announcement, the night arived. He told Pauline he had some business to take care of in town and would be home late. Pauline could have questioned him further, but that wasn't her way. She trusted him and that was enough. Buford drove the several miles alone in the pick-up truck, gaining anger as he traveled. He parked among overhanging trees, directly across from the Lucky Spot, and waited. It was a quiet night as Buford had calculated, but not too quiet for a few poor souls to be beaten or to lose a paycheck, or to be mugged and rolled for what they hadn't lost inside. He watched such an incident as he waited. One of the girls in scanty dress supported a staggering drunk on one side while Bozo the bartender held his other shoulder. About halfway to a trailer, the drunk pitched forward against the ground, passed out. After giving the drunk a prod with his foot, Bozo squatted down and removed the wallet from his trousers. Right there, in the blazing neon, he counted the money and gave part of it to the girl. They dragged the drunk into the trailer, and closed the door.

"Seems like as good a time as any," Buford said quietly. He reached beside him to the club he had so carefully fashioned. It was smooth now and rounded. It was about twice as thick around the handle as the largest big league baseball bat, that much larger at the end, and was about six inches longer than any bat a power hitter would use. Buford got out of the

49

truck, carrying the heavy piece of oak as though it were papier-mache.

He strode evenly to the front doors and let himself inside. Yes, it was a quiet night. In the bar only a single lamp lighted the area of the cash register. There were no customers in this room, and only one bar girl. Buford recognized her at once. It was Luan, the girl with the see-through blouse. She stared at him without emotion, drawing casually on her cigarette.

Buford paused a moment, knowing Bozo would soon reenter from the trailer lot. It was only a few second before he arrived. He stepped inside, threw the door latch, and took two steps. That was as far as Buford would let him go. When Bozo froze to ready himself for battle, Buford let loose with the bat. It caught Bozo mid-stomach and down he crashed. A triple, Buford thought to himself, and no outs. He swung around, walked past the stoical bar girl, and through the drapes that obscured the gaming room.

Buford knew a couple of the names by this time. The bouncer with so much apparent importance was Buel Jaggers. He was actually the operator of the game, which accounted for his fighting spirit. The man with the knife was a punk named Otie Doss. The only other name Buford knew was the nervous little man behind the cashier's cage. He was Ferrin Meaks, a manager of a Selmer loan company until the big money came his way. They were all on hand now, and for this Buford was grateful. There were also the same dealers, bouncers, the stickman and several die-hard gamblers. Among all of them, three or four of the bar girls inter-mingled.

It was dark at the doorway, and at the sound, Jaggers turned and said, "What's up, Bozo?"

Buford strolled into the light, and Jaggers nearly toppled from his high stool. "It's him. It's that son-of-a-bitch Pusser. . . . Get him!"

Otie Doss was closest, and this suited Buford just fine. Otie flipped open his switchblade and lunged forward. Buford gave his elongated bat an upward arch, and the timing was perfect. Just as Otie came into range, the bat smashed across his mouth. The knife clattered to the floor. Otis let out an anguished cry as he flopped against the nearby wall. Buford was upon him. He hoisted the smaller man in both hands and sent him through one of the black-painted windows. He picked up his club in time to greet the stickman and two of the bouncers. He caught the stickman on the shoulder and sent him to the floor beneath the dice table. He held his dangling arm in agony. Buford used his free arm to punch the other two attackers, until he could position them for the club. One of them got it in the face, then in a circling move the club caught the other on the back of the head. Buford was free when Jaggers confronted him. Jaggers wore the familiar brass knuckles, but Buford vowed he would not feel them. He let the game operator throw a wild punch, and stepped aside only at the final moment. With Jaggers off balance, Buford drew back his right fist and drove it savagely into his mouth. Jaggers flew to the wall and fell to the floor with a thump.

When another bouncer jumped on Buford's

51

back, he rammed him against the wall in a backward rush. With the body pinned behind him, Buford used his own head to batter him. Two dealers and another bouncer came into Buford's range, and he lashed out with feet and fists. He cleared the club to bring it down on one of the heads. The remaining dealer was hoisted in an airplane spin. Buford ran with him and threw him through the other painted window to the ground outside.

Jaggers, with blood spewing from nose and mouth, was once more on the attack. Now Buford was ready for his finale. The club was abandoned. He didn't need it. Buford lowered his head and charged his attacker, driving him into the wall. Quickly, he put an arm lock on him and forced him over the dice table. "Crack!" One more arm to go. Buford lifted him bodily and slammed him to the floor. He bounced on top of him, twisting the other arm behind his back. Buford pushed until: "Crack!" That was the other arm. Jaggers sobbed in pain as he thrashed about on the floor.

Buford surveyed the room. All was still except for moaning, crying, and muzzled cursing. Buford calmly retrieved his club and sauntered to the cashier's cage. En route he passed the doorway where the three bar girls hovered in silent astonishment. "Evening, ladies," he said with steady voice.

They simply stared.

Buford peered into the cubicle occupied by Ferrin Meaks. He saw a trembling, pale-faced man, seemingly on the verge of a heart attack. Buford saw the little man glance nervously at a nearby shotgun, but knew he wouldn't use it.

"I . . . I'm just the bookkeeper," said Meaks. "I had nothing to do with it."

Buford took a piece of paper from his pocket and placed it before the cashier. "This is a receipt for $3,630. $3,300 for my station wagon . . . $280 for my cash. The doctor's bill is about fifty. Please sign it, and give me the money."

Meaks took all the money from the open safe and put it before Buford in even stacks.

Buford took three of the banded thousand-dollar stacks and part of another. He pushed the rest back. "Just $3,630 is all you owe me." He tapped the receipt. "Now, sign this."

Meaks did as he was told, although signing the paper wasn't easy with his trembling fingers.

"Thank you," Buford said, when the transaction was complete.

Buford once more saw the bookkeeper eyeing the shotgun, and thought a warning might be timely. "Mr. Meaks," he said, "your hands are shaking real bad. If you happen to miss . . . you'll never shoot again."

Meaks couldn't reply. He only shook his head in agreement. Buford stuffed the money and the receipt into his pocket, took another look around, and left the Lucky Spot.

Chapter Six

Under Arrest

Buford couldn't recall an occasion where he wasn't up and active by seven in the morning, and this day was no exception. It was late when he returned home the night before, very late. Pauline was sleeping soundly, and didn't waken when Buford eased between the covers beside her. He was keyed up, but his mental exhilaration failed to postpone his needed rest. Within a few minutes he was sleeping soundly.

Buford anticipated some questions from Pauline when he woke in the morning, and she was certainly deserving of an explanation. But she didn't ask. Under the circumstances, he didn't volunteer the information either. He assumed she would find out about his postmidnight activities at the Lucky Spot sooner or later.

All Buford's trophies and possessions had been moved into his new home by this time, and it seemed a good time to try out some of his neglected weapons. Mike was delighted with his role of assistant to his father's skeet-shooting session. Buford set up the portable clay pigeon launcher, loaded it, and explained to his son how to fire the object at his command.

"Pull!" said Buford, with double-barreled shotgun poised and ready.

The clay pigeon fluttered into the sky, and Buford fired. It was a direct hit. The spray of broken clay told the story.

Buford was ready again. "Pull!" he commanded.

Buford was pleased with his aim after so long a recess, and Mike was ecstatic. "Wow, terrific, dad!" Mike said after the second shot.

But everyone wasn't as happy about the sudden reports of gunfire. Dwana sat on the kitchen steps holding her ears, and Shep ran in circles barking. When Buford was ready to call for a third launching, Pauline emerged from inside the house. Her alarm graded down to dismay and finally to anger. Buford anticipated her disapproval, and had a prepared explanation ready to offer. Guns had to be fired periodically for their own longevity, and trapshooting was a highly respected sport throughout the world. He knew her feelings about firearms, but he hoped she would begin to see things his way, even if it required time.

There was no time for reprimand from Pauline, or for Buford's calculated plea. Before either could meet for discussion, a fleet of police cruisers spun into the lower driveway. There was the black and white sheriff's car with the boldly painted lettering on the hood, and two other patrol cars. Thurman and Coker got out of the lead car and came toward Buford. The four deputies from the other cars followed with poised shotguns. Thurman and Grady Coker carried riot sticks.

"You're under arrest, Buford," said Thurman. His men formed a semicircle around Buford and Mike.

"What for?" Buford asked, making sure his shotgun was broken.

"Assault and battery and armed robbery," Thurman replied.

Pauline came into the gathering in time to hear. With her were Dwana and Shep. The dog began to growl menacingly, sensing the danger that threatened his master.

"If the dog moves . . . shoot him," Thurman said to the deputies.

"Down, Shep. Sit!" Buford commanded. Reluctantly the dog did as he was told.

"Okay, cuff him, Grady," said Thurman.

Grady looked at the sheriff and then at Pauline and the children. He hesitated for a moment, but finally complied—awkwardly—with the order. Buford offered his arms without resistance.

"Buford," Pauline said fearfully. "I . . . don't understand. What happened?"

"He knocked over the Lucky Spot is all," Thurman said sarcastically.

"Don't worry, Pauline," Buford said. "I'll be all right. Tell dad I'll be needing some bail money."

Thurman took Buford's arm and began to lead him toward the waiting cars. Dwana, in a burst of childish anger, ran after the sheriff and pushed at him from behind.

"My daddy wouldn't rob anybody!" she cried.

The sheriff looked down at the frantic child. "Violence seems to run in the family, don't it, Buford?"

Pauline took Dwana in her arms and watched helplessly as her husband was loaded into the caged rear seat of the patrol car. Buford sat still with eyes straight ahead as the cars roared out of the driveway.

Buford was uncommunicative during the booking procedures. He answered direct questions, but wasn't even slightly interested in Thurman's casual inquiries and reprimands. He would save his words for someone with intelligence. He thought the proper moment had come a couple of hours later when he faced Judge Clarke in his chambers, but this, too, was an illusion. The man made a distinguished appearance in his immaculate white linen suit, and black string tie, but it was clear where his allegiance lay. The announcement of Buford's bail told the story.

"Fifty thousand dollars bail?" Buford exclaimed. "Why they don't go that high for premeditated murder in this state. And only one day to prepare for trial? It's unconstitutional."

Strands of the judge's carefully groomed gray hair fell over his forehead in his animated exasperation. "You're ignorant of the law, Pusser," he said. "You refused to hire counsel, so you suffer the consequences of your foolishness. Do you have any idea of what you face?"

"Sure," said Buford, sharing the anger, "a frameup."

The judge brought his fist down on his desk. "A possible sentence of thirty years, that's what!" Buford expressed his shock. "Now, whether you want it or not I'm going to give you the benefit of my legal wisdom. Don't go to trial. Plead guilty to the assault charge. Make financial restitution, and I'll personally consider some kind of lesser sentence."

"How much . . . lesser?"

"I'll work that out with Sheriff Thurman," said the judge.

Buford glanced at Thurman, who had been seated on the edge of the judge's desk. He seemed pleased with the judge's suggestion.

"In that case," said Buford with finality, "I'll take my chances with a McNairy County jury."

"You're a damned fool, Buford," the judge shouted. Then he regained control. "But then, we've already established that, haven't we?"

Buford, still handcuffed, was led across the street to the County Jail. Thurman kept up a steady fusillade of warning and reprimand. "We don't take too well to troublemakers around here," he said. "Everything's nice and peaceful and you come back here and try to change things around your way. Well, you're. . . ."

"There's wrong and there's right," Buford cut in. "When the law refuses to protect the people, then the people have to act for themselves. If you had done your job, I would never have gone back to that place."

"Well, you're going to see what happens when people take the law in their own hands," Thurman said, giving Buford a push into the jail entrance. "I hope they give you *fifty* years."

"They probably will if the gamblers own the jury too, but I don't think so. The people in McNairy County know what happened down in Phoenix City, Alabama, and they saw what went on in Mississippi a few years ago. I saw plenty myself. I don't think the good people like what's going on, Thurman."

"You'll see, big mouth," Thurman said, turning Buford over to a turnkey. "You'll find out tomorrow morning . . . bright and early."

"You know what I saw down in Mississippi

when I was only seventeen, Thurman," said Buford. "I saw a bar owner—a woman—beat a sailor to death with a claw hammer. All he did was argue about the size of his check. I saw that, Thurman. I saw the sheriff afterward, too. He just laughed. A man is dead and this man of law laughs at it. That man reminds me something of you, Sheriff."

Thurman poked a finger at Buford's face, "You'll go too far, Pusser. And when you do, I'll squash you. Don't think for one minute I won't."

Buford smiled derisively as he turned to enter the barred sanctum of the jail. When the gate slid shut behind him, Thurman ordered the turnkey to put Buford in isolation. "Give him some time alone with himself," he said, "to see what a damn fool he is."

Nothing could have pleased Buford more. He had been uncomfortable among the drunks and petty thieves in the booking tank. He welcomed the isolation to plan his case. It also gave plenty of room to exercise. This he did for several grueling hours. There was nothing worse than being locked up, but something harder to take than the confinement was the deadly inactivity behind bars. He used the privacy of his cell to work himself into perspiring exhaustion. At night he phrased and rephrased what he would say in court. Finally he gave up. There was no way to plan what to say until he saw the faces of the jury. Then, he would have to rely on the words God provided. He turned over and fell asleep.

In the morning Buford was nervous. Not out of fear, but out of boredom. He was awakened at five-thirty, was given bread and coffee for breakfast, and then had nothing to do but wait for court to convene at ten. It was a long four and a half hours. Finally, he was escorted by armed deputies to the courtroom of Judge Clarke. Buford watched impassively as the proceedings took place. He was asked if he wished to challenge the jury members, but he didn't. They were men in hard hats, overalls and well-worn business suits, exactly the kind of people he had seen that day in the Lucky Spot. They looked fine to him.

He smiled at Pauline, who was seated on one of the front benches between Grandma and Grandpa, and as he looked to the rear he was surprised to see how the courtroom had filled up. Obviously word of the trial had gotten around despite the short notice. Then the crew from the Lucky Spot filed into the room. They looked as though they had just been moved to the rear after having been chewed up in the Battle of the Bulge. Buford wasn't necessarily proud of his accomplishment, only interested. Otie Doss, the man who liked switchblades, wore a cast on his jaw. The stickman appeared on crutches with a broken leg, one of the bouncers had both eyes swollen shut, another had his arm in a sling, and Buel Jaggers occupied three chairs of his own. His body cast required the space. The arms were suspended at right angles to his body, being held aloft by the plaster and metal. His cheeks and mouth were swollen to pumpkin proportions. If there was a moment when Buford felt pleased with his handiwork, it was when he saw Jaggers. Additionally, there were the bar girls, and Ferrin Meaks. The opposing team had him outnumbered, but he had fought against such odds in the past. He was still confident.

The gavel sounded. "The people of the state of Tennessee versus Buford Pusser," Sheriff Thurman droned. "Honorable Judge Homer Clarke presiding."

As the judge advised the jury of Buford's decision to act as his own counsel, a sound was heard from the rear of the room. It was Buford's father. He hurried down the aisle, and leaned over the railing to whisper into Buford's ear. "They just pulled Lutie McVeigh and his car out of the river," he said.

Buford sent an accusing glare in the direction of Jaggers. Jaggers met the stare and tried his best to produce a sardonic smile. It didn't quite come off with his painfully swollen lips. Buford drew in a sigh and nodded to his father.

"You may call your first witness," the judge said to the prosecution.

"Buel Jaggers," the district attorney announced.

Jaggers maneuvered to standing with great difficulty and inched his way to the witness stand. He grimaced with pain with every move. When he was seated, Buford heard for the first time their version of his visit to the Lucky Spot two nights earlier. The version wasn't far from the truth, so Buford offered no objections. Each subsequent witness told pretty much the same story, but in each case the emphasis was placed on a robbery motive. Nothing was mentioned about the precipitating events much earlier. The witnesses acted as though Buford had been a stranger who had charged in on them with robbery on his mind. He knew what they were doing, and exercised great patience while they did it. Finally, about midafternoon, his time arrived. The defense was put on the stand.

Buford calmly explained every detail of the earlier episode to a very attentive jury. He was careful not to show too much emotion or rancor. He was also careful to avoid exaggeration or anything that might sound that way. When he felt they were with him, he paused a moment and looked into each of their faces.

"This morning," he said, looking from one to another, "my only witness, Lutie McVeigh . . . was fished out of the river." He paused as a gasp rose from the spectators. "So they've had their say . . . and it looks to me they've had that kind of say around here too long.

"I had to stand up for myself . . . alone. No, I didn't go to rob any gambling joint with nothing but a stick. I went there to remind them that somewhere in this world there is still a little law and order left . . . to let them know, in the only terms *their* kind understands, that they couldn't buy, bribe, or threaten their way out of what they did to me . . . *this!*"

Buford rose at his own cue, and ripped his shirt from his body, sending buttons bouncing over the counsel table. He strode bare-chested before the jury, exposing the angry red slash marks that covered him from his neck to his belt. He threw his shirt on the counsel table in front of the prosecutor. He jumped to his feet in bitter protest.

"Objection, your honor. I object!"

"You're out of order!" the judge shouted at Buford, his gavel pounding furiously.

Grasping the railing in front of the panel, Buford said: "If you let them do this to me and get away with it . . . you'll be handing them the *eternal right* to do the same thing to any one of *you!*"

The judge had risen to his feet. "You're out of order! And put your shirt on!"

Buford collected his shirt and slowly got into it. When he returned to the witness stand, he said very quietly: "The defense rests, your honor."

Buford was excused from the stand and the judge gave the jury their instructions. He made clear his personal feelings by the lingering anger that accompanied his speech. He sent the jury out for deliberation. When the judge stood up to leave the bench, he sent Buford a searing glance. He then retreated to his chambers.

Buford crossed his legs in preparation for a long wait. He didn't know if he was to stay in the courtroom or leave. He decided he might as well stay there until somebody told him otherwise. Before it became important, Buford was startled by the bailiff, who called the court back in session. The judge and jury returned to the courtroom after less than five minutes of deliberation. Buford was puzzled. Was this good or bad? Had the jury been bought off by Jaggers and his bunch? For the first time he felt queasy and apprehensive; a knot seemed to tie itself in his stomach.

"Mr. Foreman," the judge said, somewhat disturbed and incredulous, "have the jurors reached a verdict?"

The jury foreman, an old, scraggly farmer in overalls, stood up and faced the court. "Yes, your honor," he said through toothless gums. "The jury finds the defendant . . . not guilty!"

The spectators gave out a unified cheer. The judge pounded his gavel. Buford was smothered by hugs and kisses from his family. As they filed out of the courtroom, Sheriff Thurman stood with hands on hips, glaring at Buford. Jaggers tried to turn in his scarecrow cast to issue a menacing leer of his own, but couldn't quite pull it off. Buford struggled through the crowd into the outside hallway as well-wishers gathered around to slap his back and shake his hand in congratulations. Obra Eaker caught up with him when he reached the hall bulletin board.

"Man," he said with a palm on Buford's shoulder, "You really know how to play to the crowd. You had that jury ready to walk barefoot over hot coals for you."

Buford grinned appreciatively.

Obra's eye caught sight of something in prominent display on the bulletin board. It was a campaign poster with Sheriff Thurman's picture. "Re-elect Al Thurman For Sheriff," it said. Obra rapped the poster with his hand, and Buford looked around at it.

"That's something they'd never do for *him*," Obra said. "Why don't you try that job on for size?"

Buford studied the poster thoughtfully.

Pauline overheard Obra's remark, but didn't say anything. It all came into focus that evening at home. "Buford," she said, sitting on the arm of his easy chair. "You didn't take all that seriously, did you? I mean what Obra was saying."

"You mean, am I going to run for sheriff?"

She nodded.

"Yes, Pauline," he said, thankful for the opportunity to put it into words. "I think I just might."

"No, Buford, NO!" she cried. "We'll go someplace else . . . find a decent town to live in."

"Where? How?" Buford said, taking her hands in his. "Every cent we had is tied up in this place. I never ran with my tail between my legs before . . . and I'm not going to start now."

Pauline moved from his grasp and turned away. "Is your pride worth the safety of the children . . . of all of us?"

"Maybe *you* should leave," said Buford calmly. "Go to your family with the kids until it's safe to come back."

She faced him again imploringly. "I don't want to leave you . . . and I don't want you to run for sheriff. No more fighting, you said. You gave your *word* . . . Wild Bull Buford's word . . . that you can bank on."

Buford sighed. He felt a pang of guilt. "You're right," he said. "But I didn't know this was going to happen."

"And you're making it into a senseless life and death grudge fight."

"Senseless?" Buford stood up. "Now, Pauline, you listen to me. This is my home . . . and you've made it yours. Do you want you and me, and Mike and Dwana hiding all our lives . . . afraid to come home?"

Pauline was pleading with him, something Buford had never known her to do. She held his hand in both of hers. "Just for a while," she said, tears welling in her eyes. "Only until this violence blows over."

"It's not going to blow over by itself," he reasoned. "Somebody's got to huff and puff to make it blow over. I think I can win that election, Pauline. And I know I've got to try."

"But what if you don't win?" she said. "Then you'd be worse off than before. Who would stand up for you against them, if you lost the election?"

"Okay," said Buford with a faint grin. "If I lose the election we'll leave. But *only then* . . . fair enough?"

Pauline fell into his arms and they held each other. In a moment she pushed back and was smiling. "You couldn't lose that election and you know it," she said, with all protest diminished. "It'll be Buford the Bull in three straight falls, so I might as well get used to it."

"That's more like my girl talking," said Buford enclosing her again in his arms. "But it's going to be all right . . . I promise . . . Buford's word."

Chapter Seven

The New Candidate

Although Sheriff Thurman and Judge Clarke tried their hardest to suppress the news of Buford's quick and victorious trial, the newspapers picked it up almost immediately. It was as though everyone in the County had been biding their time for someone like Buford to happen along; a man who could harness the growing community anger and put it into action. From the moment Buford announced his candidacy, he had an instant army of supporters.

He was enjoying it, too: his campaign. He turned it into a battle of wits, and used it to infuriate Thurman into miscues. After a few weeks of Buford's calculated harassment, Thurman couldn't conduct a speech without becoming so vitriolic he turned people away. No opposing candidate could be as worthless, corrupt, and evil as the picture he painted of Buford. It was so totally black, no one except Thurman's staunchest supporters could believe it. This amused Buford greatly.

One day at the mill, Buford's father drew him aside, and Buford knew a lecture was in the offing. When the stage was properly set, his father eased into the subject. "That Thurman," he said massaging his chin in deepest thought. "He's been saying some pretty bad things about you, son. People are wonderin' why you don't hit back at him . . . or at least deny all them charges."

Buford laughed. "Why, pa, if I didn't know you so well, I'd be wondering if *you* believed what he's saying."

"You know better than that. It's just that he's gettin' awful dirty, and it can't do you any harm to at least come out and call him a liar."

"I call him corrupt, bought-and-paid-for, self-serving, and a habitual liar," said Buford, still amused. "In every speech I've made I've tied him in with the gamblers and moonshiners. I think that should get it done. The point is, if he's a liar as I charge, then how could what he's saying be accepted as true? If the people believe me, they can't very well believe him."

"I see your point, I guess, but I still wish you would answer all those trumped-up charges he's making."

"I was thinking I might publish a big ad just before election," said Buford. "Every charge he's made against me, I'll turn it back to him. But I guess I can't include the one about my being kicked out of the Marine Corps on a Section Eight; the Marines wouldn't have anyone like him in the first place."

"Section Eight means they let you go 'cuz you was crazy, don't it?"

"Uh huh, something like that. But don't worry, pa, I'll show him how crazy I am by election time . . . I'll be crazy all right . . . crazy like a fox."

One of Buford's favorite tricks was to look for Thurman campaign posters. Where it said: "VOTE FOR," on the top of the sign, Buford added a single word printed in identical type.

68

The word was: "DON'T". Then he would place his own poster below Thurman's.

He wasn't taking the election that lightly, but knowing Thurman's temperament, the psychology had its desired effect. It drove Thurman wild. He and his deputies would cruise the County looking for Buford's handiwork. While he was doing this, Buford would be conducting campaign calls. He had little faith in poster advertising anyway.

Finally, during the last days of the campaign, Thurman began to work much closer to Buford, almost following his every move. It seemed he was worried, too. Reports were that he had been drinking more heavily than usual, and this was fine with Buford. One afternoon, Buford was well aware of Thurman's close follow-up. He would see the sheriff car pull into every spot he visited just moments after he pulled out. A face-to-face encounter finally took place at Willie Rae Lockman's bar.

Buford had just finished tacking up a few signs in the all-Negro establishment, and was talking to a few of the scantily dressed bar girls, when Thurman, obviously drunk, charged into the darkened room. Behind him was Grady Coker, carrying a stack of posters, tacks, and a hammer. In red-faced fury, Thurman snatched a poster from Grady, placed it over Buford's sign, and held it there for Grady to drive the tacks. With that accomplished, he nailed two other posters on the wall, and looked to Buford with a triumphant glare.

Buford grinned at the childish behavior, rested his everpresent oak club over his shoulder and started out the door.

"Hey, Buford!" Thurman shouted after him. "How would you like a nice, plush job as my deputy? No brains required . . . just brute animal force."

Buford turned back long enough to look coldly into Thurman's eyes. "I'm not that desperate," he said.

Grady placed a restraining hand on Thurman's shoulder, but the sheriff would have none of it. He pushed the hand off and rushed out the door after Buford. He paused in the doorway to yell: "You *will* be, boy!" He laughed wildly. "You sure as hell will be . . . day after election!"

Buford paid little attention to his drunken opponent. He was more preoccupied with the scene outside the bar. There was a series of battered house trailers, which seemed to be standard equipment for such places, but in this case the accouterments were cheaper and shabbier. As he counted out some campaign signs, a pretty black girl led a stumbling black companion into one of the trailers. This place would go too, he thought to himself . . . right after election.

Thurman cupped his hands when Buford started to get into his car. "Last chance, Buford!" he droned bitterly. "If you can't beat 'em, join 'em!"

Buford had had enough of Thurman's drunken yelling. He started his car, and in his departure from the lot his back wheels threw cinders.

"Aha, you see that, Grady?" Thurman said pointing at the swiftly departing car. "That's what I call reckless driving. That boy's just got no respect for law and order."

Thurman nearly fell as he hurried down the

steps. He righted himself, and rushed to the cruiser in unsteady strides.

"Al!" Grady pleaded. "Let him go."

"Goddammit, Grady . . . you act like you're gonna vote for him! Get in the car or I'll dock you a day's pay."

Grady just made it, Thurman bucked the car into action, and roared after Buford with Grady's door still open. Grady gripped the side post to keep from falling out.

With the car bouncing on and off the small lane that led to the highway, Thurman began to laugh crazily. "We'll get him. We'll get him, Grady . . . and we'll nail his ass to the cross!"

Buford watched the erratic cruiser in his rearview mirror. He wondered just how far Thurman might go. It looked as though he would soon find out.

The Sheriff's blinker light went on simultaneously with the siren, but Buford decided against stopping—at least out here in the country. Considering Thurman's intake of alcohol, blended with his natural bad temper, Buford thought it best to have witnesses present if there should be a physical encounter. He increased his own speed.

Buford was convinced more than booze was at work inside Thurman's brain. He had obviously gone mad. His lights blinked on and off and the white and black cruiser swerved in pursuit. Suddenly the cruiser burst in a surge of speed, and bumped the rear of Buford's car. He fought the wheel to right himself, again and again he felt the jolt of the pursuing vehicle. It was hard enough keeping his car on the road, but Buford considered other possibilities.

71

One of these times, Thurman would start shooting and Buford wanted to see it in time to duck. So he was traveling a narrow and winding county road at better than sixty miles an hour, was constantly getting bumped from behind, and had to keep his eyes on the road while checking the rearview mirror. He was almost relieved when Thurman swerved his car into the oncoming land and drew abreast of him. He thought the cruiser would pass him, and Buford started to slow. But too late.

Directly ahead of both cars was a narrow, steel-beamed bridge. It would be impossible for both vehicles to clear it—not at this speed. Buford glanced into the wavering cruiser to see Thurman in a state of exhilaration. He was waving his fist and laughing crazily. Buford quickly double sticked into second gear. As he was doing it, the cruiser lurched to the right and bumped Buford's car. Buford gave his car the gun and shot ahead. The emergency speed was barely sufficient, but he was able to swerve in front of the cruiser and cross the bridge safely. He kept the pedal to the floor to enlarge the distance between him and Thurman, and waited for the crossroads he knew was straight ahead. Without reducing speed, Buford waited until the road was yards away, then he hit the brakes, geared down and spun into the roadway. Thurman, taken by surprise, sped past.

Buford stalled out as he screeched to a stop, but restarted in an instant. He jammed the car into reverse and screeched back to the highway to head in the opposite direction. He dug out as fast as the car would carry him in the direction of the bridge. He could see Thurman's wild U-turn and knew the cruiser would be upon him in moments. He hadn't had time for much thought until now, but in this brief respite from attack he arrived at a decision. He was through running.

After passing the bridge, Buford pulled to the side and stopped. He took up his club, and got out of the car. He saw the racing cruiser approach him and the bridge, and walked toward it. Buford had no way of calculating his present odds; there was no time for arithmetic. He only knew he had to face the challenge.

Then an unexpected break. The curve before the bridge was too much for Thurman to handle. The cruiser careened, braked and swerved broadside in the center of the road. It straightened again, but immediately fishtailed. As it spun, the rear end smashed against the bridge abutment and the car plunged over the side of the bank. Buford watched helplessly as the cruiser burst into flame and came to rest in the river below.

Buford ran down the embankment, stumbling, sliding, but the car was on its side totally engulfed in flame. He paused a moment, believing both men were trapped inside, but then he saw a form come to the surface, face down. It was Grady. Buford plunged into the river.

Leaning away from the intense heat, Buford lifted Grady's head above water, and put a finger inside his mouth to pull the tongue from his throat. He could see now that Grady's leg was caught under the rear bumper. He arched Grady over his back and reached down to free the leg. Moments later he was able to drag Grady to the river bank. When Grady began to cough his way to consciousness, Buford plunged back into the water to make an attempt to get to Thurman on the opposite side of the car. He stopped midway. The heat was too intense to go further, but he was also aware that Thurman could never have survived this long. It was hopeless.

He returned to the bank where Grady was now sitting up, breathing more easily. "I couldn't help Thurman," Buford said, with genuine regret.

"I know," said Grady. "You were a fool to come out after me."

"You okay?" Buford asked, flopping beside him on the bank.

Grady nodded. "Thanks to you, I am."

"I should've stopped before," Buford said.

"I don't blame you," Grady said. "I've never seen Al that crazy before. He probably would have shot you."

Buford sighed, refusing to watch the flaming car. "Guess that's something we'll never know."

Chapter Eight

Buford Pusser: Sheriff

For every dead man there should be at least one mourner, and in the case of Sheriff Al Thurman there were several. But the group that gathered the next day at the Green Lantern Bar were shedding no tears. The death of their favorite sheriff was a great personal loss, and more than a minor inconvenience. Their solution to the problem finally arrived, and without preamble, stacks of hundred dollar bills were placed on the bar.

The remuneration was for services to be rendered by Grady Coker, who sat staring at the means of instant wealth. He was surrounded by every game operator, bar owner, and tinhorn gambler in the county. There was also a contingent of moonshiners sitting toward the back of the room who had contributed to the fund.

Jaggers, still unable to sit comfortably, stood next to Grady with his coat draped over his two broken shoulders. He was perplexed by Grady's lack of enthusiasm, and his anger was rising.

"Dammit, Grady," he said. "That's more money than you can make in twenty years as a deputy. All you gotta do is testify that Buford deliberately ran you off the road. That's murder . . . and the end of him."

Grady drained the can of beer, and stood up from the bar. "I'll think it over," he said.

The first to challenge him was Augie McCullah, a red-haired and fiery-tempered moonshiner who was used to getting his own way. He grabbed Grady by the shirt. "Don't give us that think-it-over crap, Grady!" he said. "You'll do it . . . or else!"

Grady's reaction stunned the bargainers. He lifted a knee into Augie's groin, doubling him over. Then he drove the other knee into Augie's face. He sprawled backwards on the floor. Grady drew his gun and backed away.

"I'd be dead if it weren't for Buford," he said fiercely. "So just stay out of my way!"

When he started toward the door, a pair of bouncers moved into his path. Grady eyed them coldly, and without warning, fired a round between them. They stepped aside hastily, and he left the room. His departure was followed by a moment of grim silence.

Callie Hacker, owner of the Green Lantern and a fading beauty with cold green eyes, slapped a palm on the bar. "I'll be damned!" she said, shaking her head. "How do you figure people?"

Augie struggled to his feet, trying to cover his humiliation with epithets. "Why, that punk turncoat . . . that tin-badged creep! I'll fix him . . . I'll see that he . . ."

"There is no time for that," Callie interrupted. "Our only chance now is to elect a corpse. We'll put up some big billboards, and buy radio and TV spots, calling in all favors owed to us."

Augie thought for a moment and nodded. "You're right, Callie," he said. "Let's throw everything we can lay our hands on behind our late sheriff. Another ten or twenty thousand should do it."

shirt and slacks—and carried no weapon beyond his trademark: the big stick.

"Two rules," said Buford, looking the men over. "That's all . . . and don't forget them. One: we enforce the law equally. Two: any man who takes a bribe will get his head knocked off . . . by me. Now, Grady's going to show me the territory, and. . . ."

The sound of a barking radio broke his train of thought.

"Two-oh-one calling five-oh-one," said the voice. "Two-oh-one to five-oh-one. Come in if you can hear me."

"That's you, Sheriff," said Grady, "five-oh-one."

Buford acknowledged Grady's solution to the mystery, and slid behind the wheel of the new car. He unhooked the microphone and pushed the talk switch. "This is five-oh-one," said Buford. "Who are you?"

"This is Sheriff Tanner over in Alcorn, Mississippi," said the voice over the radio. "Welcome to the shooting gallery. Hate to give you a big one first morning on the job, but we've got a multiple death case over here that might interest you."

"Be there in an hour, Sheriff," said Buford.

"No rush. We've got 'em on ice . . . over."

"I'll still be there in an hour," Buford said. "Over and out."

Within the hour, Buford was escorted into a small white room where there were four corpses stretched out on autopsy tables. Four others were laid out on the floor. All were covered with rubber sheets. Buford looked them over with the help of the attendant. A moment later,

Sheriff Tanner entered the room with a middle-aged Negro prisoner.

"It was a civil rights picnic," said Tanner. "All young . . . in their early twenties. Got a dozen more in County Hospital. All victims of poisoned white lightning."

Tanner approached the prisoner and put a hand under his chin to lift his face. "This here's Sheriff Pusser from McNairy County," he said to the frightened Negro. "Tell him where you picked up that lot of moonshine . . . and don't lie."

"From Willie Rae Lockman," he mumbled. "At his bar over near Selmer."

After leaving Alcorn, Buford's first inclination was to go directly to Lockman's bar, but he changed his mind. He settled on an alternate course, one that could have a double purpose. He drove west of town to the farm belonging to Obra Eaker's father.

The place hadn't changed since Buford was a boy. The shack and barn were still devoid of paint, and were a good windstorm away from collapsing. The fields were overgrown with weeds, and a few chickens strutted around the debris-ridden farm yard. Buford spotted Obra's truck near the barn, and then saw that Obra was there working on it. He appeared to be in the early stages of a complete engine overhaul. As Buford parked, an ancient Negro stepped out of the house carrying a shotgun. Obra waved him back inside.

"Mornin', Sheriff," said Obra, wiping his hands on a rag. "My, you sure do look the part."

"Obra, your friend Willie Rae Lockman runs

a still back up here someplace. Know where it is?"

"Wow! You are some quick study," said Obra angrily. "You got the dialogue, the coldness, the official manner down to a T."

Buford couldn't alter his feelings for friendship. "I came directly from the morgue over in Alcorn," he said coldly. "They got eight niggers stretched out. All dead from poisoned whiskey made and sold here. Now let's not waste time playing word games."

"Hold it . . . you don't talk to me like that, Buford!"

"Well, you been talking all over the county about helping your people. I'm giving you the chance." Buford paused a moment. "Obra . . . the last sheriff wouldn't have given a damn about those eight bodies, because they weren't his favorite color. I care . . . and I'm going to do something about it whether you help me or not."

Obra's anger waned with Buford's somber message. "They're working about seven miles back up there in those hills near an old logging road . . . some guys from Arkansas. I'll show you."

"Thanks," said Buford, as coldly as before. "I've got something for you."

He went to his car, and Obra watched in silence. For the moment there was a communications failure. But Buford began to clear the channels when he brought out a gun belt and badge. He returned to Obra. "What I got for you is a new job," said Buford. "Deputy Sheriff of McNairy County."

Obra swallowed and took a backward step.

"Buford you . . . you've been away too long. That just isn't *done* around here."

"Is that so? It's all right for you to set up a white trash wrestler for sheriff . . . but it's not good enough for *you*, huh?"

Buford slapped the gun belt into Obra's hands, and stuck the badge to his shirt pocket.

"Easy as that, eh?" said Obra, grinning.

"That's all there is to it . . . if you know the right people."

Obra was bewildered by his instantaneous change of vocation, but he left his disassembled truck engine behind and got into the new cruiser with Buford. They drove to an old logging road in the hills, and by the time they parked beneath some willow trees, Obra had strapped on the gun belt and had refastened the badge more securely. He led the way through the thick foliage. Buford followed with his big stick.

After more than a mile of hiking, they came to a bend in the footpath. Obra signaled for Buford to be quiet. Buford eased beside him and observed the activity in the clearing below. They saw a still with several barrels that were filled with mash and water. There was a new car and an old flatbed truck loaded with a copper kettle and several cartons of jars. Five shirtless Negroes were at work around the still, all of them covered with grime and dust. Buford motioned for Obra to come in from the opposite side. He climbed through the brush to comply, as Buford strolled boldly into the clearing.

"You're all under arrest," he said evenly. "Stay where you are."

Willie Rae Lockman was carrying a box of

moonshine. At the sound of Buford's voice, he set it down on the flatbed of the truck. Buford took a bottle from the box and unscrewed the cap. He took a swig, washed it around in his mouth and spat it out.

"Who owns this truck?" he asked Lockman.

The Negro's eyes edged toward the front. Buford followed his gaze and spotted a pair of feet protruding from the cab. He walked past Willie Rae, and took careful aim with his club. He cracked it against the soles of the shoes. With a howl of pain, Augie McCullah danced to the ground. His nap had been rudely interrupted.

"Who the hell's the smart. . . ." His mouth remained open but the words failed at the sight of Buford.

Buford pointed his stick at the flatbed containing the case of liquor. "McCullah," he said. "This truck is hereby confiscated for carrying unlicensed liquor."

Augie reacted with a look of disgust and anger but said nothing. Buford ignored his silent disdain and moved on to the new sedan. It was loaded with whiskey. He sampled the contents of another jug, and spit it out.

"Whose car is this?"

"Never saw it before," Willie Rae answered.

"Well, whoever it belongs to, they just lost it," said Buford. "And, Augie and Willie Rae . . . I forgot to tell you . . . you're both under arrest for manslaughter . . . eight counts." Obra had been in the background until now. Buford looked at him. "I'll radio Selmer for some deputies to take this truck and car back to town. Don't lose anybody."

With Buford leaving the scene, Obra suddenly remembered his gun. He nervously drew it, and used it to motion with. "Put . . . uh . . . your hands on your head, and sit down," he told Augie.

When he was certain Buford was out of hearing range, Augie said, "You showed him how to get up here, didn't you, boy?"

"I sure hope you try something, Augie," Obra said, cocking his gun.

"You *live long* enough, you're gonna wish this day never happened, smart ass."

Buford had an eventful first day as sheriff of McNairy County. He was called in to investigate a multiple homicide; he hired a black deputy; raided a group of moonshiners; and when he paraded them before the judge for arraignment, he had everything thrown back into his face.

"Sheriff Pusser," said Judge Clarke vehemently, "the court orders you to set the prisoners free."

"You can't mean that, Judge!"

"I do, and I'm so ordering you!"

"Why?"

"Because you acted improperly," said the judge. "You failed to get search and seizure warrants before you invaded their privacy. You failed to inform them at the time of their arrests of their legal rights to counsel, to silence, to access to a telephone."

"They were responsible for *eight* deaths!" Buford raged. "And are you telling me that because of some little technicalities they can. . . ."

The judge interrupted. "The United States

Supreme Court does not regard them as *little technicalities*," he said sarcastically. "Sheriff Pusser, that is the *law of the land!* There is more to upholding the law than swinging a big stick and kicking down doors. Now set them free . . . or I'll hold you in contempt . . . which I do, anyway."

Buford was so outraged he could have committed murder on his own, but he swallowed, drew in a breath, and reluctantly unlocked the handcuffs. Wide grins were worn by the freed prisoners, who enjoyed Buford's embarrassment.

Buford remained at the bench until the prisoners had filed out of the courtroom. "You just won a battle, Judge Clarke," Buford said in full control, "but don't bet that you'll win the war. I'm learning faster than you think."

The judge glared at Buford and started to mouth a reply, but reconsidered. He gnashed his teeth and withdrew to his chambers.

Chapter Nine

Clean-up Campaign

Buford acknowledged that he had much to learn in his new role as County Sheriff, and he was aware of his blunder in making the arrest at the still, but that didn't make his humiliation any easier to swallow. The trouble was, there was practically no one he could rely on for assistance. The underworld machine made sure he was strictly on his own. That was fine, he decided. He would do it on his own, and wouldn't owe anyone anything. He was convinced it was only a matter of time until the tide began to turn his way. The biggest problem was his own impatience. Buford had never been one to bide his time.

A few days later, he drove into the county parking lot where Grady was adjusting the flashed lights on his cruiser. Buford waved as he got out of his car, and started toward the rear entrance of the sheriff's department. Grady stopped what he was doing and came to him.

"A man named Witter from Nashville was here looking for you, Buford," he said. "He went up to talk to the judge."

Buford considered the message, and mopped his forehead with a handkerchief. Before he could make further inquiry, a rather heavy man in an immaculate seersucker suit appeared at the doorway. Without being told, Buford knew this was Witter. No one from McNairy County County bothered to dress that carefully.

Grady made the introductions, and disappeared. Witter grinned effusively, and clamped a hand on Buford's shoulder. Buford was immediately on his guard. He didn't like being mauled by anyone, and certainly not by strangers.

"It's certainly a pleasure to finally make your acquaintance," said Witter. "Judge Clarke's been telling me all about you."

"Shouldn't have taken him long," said Buford.

"I'd like to have a little talk with you, Pusser . . . in private."

Buford motioned to the nearby plain black cruiser.

"Perhaps your office would be better," said Witter.

"This is it."

Witter got into the car, and Buford began to drive. Witter limited his discussion to generalities until the town was several miles behind. Then he asked Buford if they could park somewhere. Buford drove to the top of a lonely road that overlooked the entire valley. He got out of the car—with his big stick in his hand—and went to the edge of the hill. Witter followed.

"Pusser," said Witter, "you're a local sheriff . . . and a new one at that. Maybe nobody told you that this is more than a local operation. There are some very important people involved . . . all the way up to the state capital . . . and beyond. I hope you'll believe this, because it's quite true."

"The only people that are *important* to me," said Buford, "are down there. They built this county and have to live in it."

"First thing you have to learn in life is to take care of number one, that's you, Buford." There was that hand again caressing Buford's shoulder. "If you don't, no one else will. And you don't have to commit any sins. All you have to do is let those who want to pay for their fun ... do it." Buford nodded thoughtfully. Actually he was remembering his earlier thoughts regarding the lack of cooperation among his associates. Suddenly he had a friend—a total stranger—who was more than willing to help him out.

"I got nothing against a drink," Buford said quietly, "or a little fun, but the law of the land shouldn't be up for sale. If you give the people who run those places an inch, they'll eventually steal the whole state." He smiled wryly. "And it looks like they already got a leg up on that."

The hand was back. "I suggest you think about it for a day or two. Come on up to Nashville. Meet the boys. You'll like them ... especially when you find out how generous they are."

"I thought it over long before I went after this job, Mr. Witter."

"So I've heard. But ideals and reality are a long way apart. One day you'll see it. And if you don't ... someone's going to point it out to you ... *clearly*."

Buford let his eyes grind pulp of Witter's face, but then managed a controlled smile. "You already have," he said. "And I thank you."

It seemed as though Mr. Witter's visit served as an activator. Buford lost no time in striking out wherever a hit was needed. With warrants almost impossible to get, he had a plan of his own. He and several deputies raided the Lucky Spot in full daylight. Every slot machine and piece of gambling paraphernalia was loaded on a truck. Buford stood by with his big stick.

Grady, puzzled, said: "No warrant, no case. Guess you know that, Buford."

Buford nodded, and strolled closer to the truck. In a sudden flurry of action, he went to work with his club. He smashed every table, dice basket, and the glass fronts of all the slot machines. "So we'll lose the case," Buford said, nodding back to the ruined equipment. "Let 'em sue me."

During the evening of the same day, Buford and his deputies visited the Green Lantern Bar. It was his first visit to the establishment owned by the notorious Callie Hacker. When Buford entered, a girl was in the process of dragging a drunk toward the front door. At the sight of Buford she detoured back to a booth. Several other hustlers were drinking at the bar with their male companions. Callie was circulating among them.

"The gal behind the bar is Callie," Grady said quietly. "That's Prentiss tending bar—her boyfriend."

Buford nodded, but he already knew Callie Hacker from a long, long time ago. It was only her name that was new to him. The last time he saw her she was hacking a sailor to death with a claw hammer. That was during his first visit to the vice dens of Mississippi when he was maybe seventeen. He wouldn't forget that face no matter how many years passed, and he was strangely pleased to face her again. Callie Hacker was filed firmly in his mind for future reference.

Buford went to a pair of slot machines near the bar. He tapped them with his club. "Load 'em up," he said.

As the deputies carried out his order, he strolled the length of the bar to another pair of familiar faces. It was the big-busted youngster named Margie Ann, and the girl with the see-through blouse, Luan Paxton.

"Evening, Luan," he said. "See you moved your trailer."

She seemed surprised at the personal greeting but immediately recaptured her cool. "Flattered you're still looking," she said, drawing on her cigarette.

"Evening, Callie," he said, glancing behind the bar. Then he looked to the bartender. "Prentiss."

In the silent room, Buford surveyed the girls and their hapless victims. "You know, Callie," he said, "you've got one of the sexiest track teams I ever saw. What's their record between here and the trailers?"

Callie's green eyes were noncommittal, but the hatred was built-in. Buford continued his stroll to the end of the bar and behind it. He poked under the bar with his club. He then paused in front of the door that obviously led to the storage room.

"Open it up," he said pointing the big stick. "The one with the illegal liquor."

Callie's eyes blazed. She looked to Buford, to Prentiss, and finally gave a long, hard look to Grady. "Prentiss," she said. "Open the door for the sheriff."

90

The bartender opened the door and led Buford into the back room. Callie leaned over the bar to speak to Grady. "You better get word to that shit, Grady," she said, spitting out the words. "He's driving the wrong way on a one-way street." Grady met her stare and held it.

Buford's clean-up campaign resulted in the second summit meeting of the local underworld in as many weeks. Before, their mission was to keep Buford from becoming elected sheriff, now, it was a matter of getting him out of their hair at any cost. This time the meeting place was the Lucky Spot, where Jaggers held reign.

Jaggers' henchmen were setting up a new dice table, and had brought new slot machines into the gaming room before the meeting began. They paused in their task when Jaggers began to speak.

"We've taken as much as anybody can take from one man," he said. "We've reasoned, we've threatened, we've offered to make the bastard rich. I say, if he won't buy off, let's kill the son of a bitch!"

Callie Hacker had taken a seat on the dice table. She tossed a pair of dice across the table and they came up snake eyes. She wasn't watching the dice, however; she was too intent on what Jaggers was saying.

"You know what Witter said," she reminded. "Go easy. The papers in Nashville are playin' up that big stick of his like he was Sir Lancelot, or somethin'."

"We ought to take that stick," said Augie McCullah, "and shove it right up his ass . . . all the way."

"We ought to do what we're told to do," said Callie. "Find some way to teach him a lesson. After that, maybe Witter can talk some sense into him."

Jaggers reacted with a sneer. "You teach him *your* kind of lesson," he said. "I've got some boys in Alabama that will teach him something he won't live to remember."

Callie threw the dice again and once again crapped out. This time she rolled a pair of sixes, and she saw the results of her roll. It played back as a bad omen. "You know I've had a lifetime of trouble, and always was able to handle it." She gazed at the fallen dice musingly. "But there's something about this guy that has me stymied. He's trouble . . . real trouble."

Jaggers made a sharp move in reaction to her words. His casts were off but both arms were held in slings. He grimaced with pain, and the pain made him angrier. "He's nothing but an overgrown flesh-and-blood man!" he exploded. "He's no god. We've been hurt plenty by that two-bit, second-rate wrestler, and now we've got to even the score. We'd better stop him . . . or he'll damn well ruin every last one of us. I say we handle things my way!"

While the argument ensued, Obra Eaker was paying one of his regular visits to Lockman's Bar. Willie Rae chose to miss today's meeting of the other operators. He had enough money problems without handing over his profits to them. When he saw Obra enter the bar, he wondered if his decision had been wise.

Obra, in his new khaki uniform and trooper's hat, leaned against the bar watching a cream-colored beauty belting out a country and western tune. She was accompanied by a three-piece rock group. Several couples were dancing seductively on the postage-stamp dance floor and, for the hour, the place was quite crowded.

Willie Rae moved along the bar to where Obra was standing. "This is the third time you've rousted me today, Obra," he said, woefully. "Why the hell you working to hurt me, brother?"

"I'm not looking to hurt *you*, Willie Rae," said Obra. "Just making sure nobody else gets hurt."

"Or maybe it's another way of sayin' you want to make a deal . . . okay?"

Obra's smile held a touch of warning. "I'm just a little deputy, Willie Rae, I don't have the authority to deal."

Obra was too involved with Willie Rae to notice the new arrivals when they entered, but six white men stumbled into the bar. They were dressed in Levi's and bright-colored shirts, and were obviously looking for trouble. The leader had a puffy face with reddish complexion, and had a prominent pot-belly. When he saw Obra, he gave one of his cronies a jab in the ribs. They moved to the bar.

"Well now," said the leader. "Saw your car outside. Thought we'd come in and pay our respects to our new deputy." He exchanged glances with his chums. "Hey, gang, look at the solid gold badge this ole boogie's wearin'."

Obra felt a stab of fear in his belly. He knew the man by name and reputation. It was Arno Purdy, and he always meant trouble.

"Now that you got yourself a steady job," Arno went on, "how about buyin' us a beer?"

Arno plunked a pint of whiskey on the bar. Obra started to back away, but Arno caught him by the shirt. To make room, he elbowed another black man off a stool along with his girl. They both fell to the floor.

"Get the hell away from the bar!" he yelled after them, as they scrambled out of his range. "Give us men some drinking room." He still held Obra's shirt collar, and gave him a shake. "Obra, I was talkin' to you, boy. You just gotta be more respectful to your betters."

Obra felt his throat tighten with fear, but he overcame it long enough to break the grasp. He ran for the door. He heard the drunks jeer after him as he ran. Outside, Obra ran to his cruiser and jumped inside. Frantically he fumbled with the mike until it was operable. "Calling five-oh-one," he said breathlessly. "This is patrol car number three calling Sheriff's car five-oh-one."

A few endless moments later, Obra breathed a deep sigh of relief.

"Five-oh-one, here," said the familiar voice. "That you, Obra?"

"Yes, Sheriff," he said. "I'm at Lockman's Bar. There are six troublemakers down here. Do you want to come down and pick them up?"

After a pause: "You pick 'em up. Haven't had lunch yet."

Obra gulped. "But . . . but they're white men . . . Arno Purdy and his bunch." Obra breathed heavily as he waited out another long pause. "You hear, Buford? They're white men."

"Obra," said Buford's voice, "you're a deputy sheriff for McNairy County, not a shoeshine boy. If they're out of line, pick them up. You need help, call the office."

Obra's heart was pounding furiously, and he had nothing wet in his mouth to swallow, but Buford's message was clear enough. He was telling him he was being a coward, and this was a chance to prove himself. Obra could think of ten million things he would rather do, but he straightened his shoulders, said a little prayer, and headed back to the bar.

Buford was a little upset with Obra for calling, and started into Elsie's kitchen for lunch. He stood in the doorway a moment, thought it over, and decided he had been wrong. He hurried back to his cruiser, jolted it into action, and spun it around on a speeding course toward Lockman's Bar. The time passed slowly over the several-mile drive, and the longer it took, the more worried he became. He would never forgive himself if Obra got himself stabbed or shot. He expected too much of people, always. This was a flaw he would have to overcome if he were to be successful as sheriff.

Buford negotiated the last rocky lane that fed into the Lockman Bar parking area, his wheels throwing an avalanche of gravel. He squealed the car to a stop, with a cloud of dust closing in. Buford ran through the dust toward the front of the building, but slowed to a stop as he turned the corner. He let his club rest at his side. The situation was under control.

He saw Obra backing out of the bar with his gun drawn. He was dragging the handcuffed Arno Purdy backwards as he moved. Purdy's five cronies followed in single file. Obra's shirt was in shreds, and he appeared a bit wobbly, but he didn't need Buford's help.

"Don't . . . don't make me kill anyone," Obra said, shakily. "Just keep moving . . . easy does it."

When he reached his car, Obra reached behind to find the latch for the back door. He finally found it, and quickly stuffed Arno inside and shut the door. He then stood where he was awaiting the approaching men.

The men seemed to be moving in a semicircle around Obra, which was beginning to make him apprehensive. He would point his gun at a man to his left, and then quickly to his right. Buford suppressed a smile, and sauntered into the scene swinging his stick. He hadn't been seen because he had parked at the opposite end of the lot, but he was seen now. The moment he appeared the five men froze as statues.

"Now, that wasn't so hard, was it?" he said to Obra.

"Not from where you were standing," Obra said.

Buford grinned and peeked into the caged patrol car at a very battered Arno Purdy. "Howdy, Arno," he said lightly.

Arno, angry and sullen and bleeding from a bump on his forehead, sat glaring straight ahead.

Chapter Ten

The "Game" Was Murder

All legal procedures were observed in the arrest and booking, so Buford appeared in court the next morning with confidence. He and Obra shared the witness stand while they described the nature of the arrest to Judge Clarke. He listened with feigned boredom, and when the case was stated, he sent separate looks of disgust to Buford and his deputy.

The judge stood up to speak. "Ten dollars or ten days," he said with a pound of the gavel. That was that. He withdrew to his chambers.

Arno and his banged-up buddies shuffled out of the courtroom. Obra sighed wearily. "Take your life in your hands for a ten dollar bill!"

"The fine isn't too important," said Buford, philosophically. "It's the principle that counts. You earned public respect."

Obra shook his head. "Come on out to my place tonight and watch the bonfire."

Buford started to say something more, but was distracted. Arno pushed his pals aside near the door and started back toward the bench. Buford might have been on guard had it not been that Arno appeared to be uneasy, embarrassed. He waited curiously.

Arno paused and scratched his head. "Uh . . . I been thinking this over all mornin'," he said sheepishly. "Hell, no use lyin' . . . I was drunk and made a fool out of myself yesterday. Had no reason under the sun for bein' at Lockman's." He had been staring everywhere but at a face. Now he looked directly into Obra's eyes. "Obra, I want you to know I'm damned sorry." Then to Buford: "Believe me, Sheriff, I mean it . . . I am." He reached into his pocket and brought out some money. "Here's twenty bucks for the shirt. Best I can do." He stuffed the money into the pocket of Obra's new shirt and quickly walked away.

Obra's mouth dropped. Buford watched with a bemused smile. He said to Obra: "Don't you just hate people like that?"

"Uh, what do you mean?"

"Just ruined our plans for the bonfire."

Obra had been had. He shook his head, and concealed his grin of concession.

Buford excused himself and headed for Judge Clarke's chambers. He knocked politely on the door, and was told to enter. The judge seemed uneasy about the unexpected visit, but did his best to appear civil.

"Uh, what can I do for you . . . Sheriff?" he said. His eyes danced over Buford's countenance to read his mood.

Buford sat on the corner of the desk, and only then did his anger surface. "That fight yesterday was for real!" he said, leaning close to the judge. "Obra could have been *killed*. And all *you* levy is a ten-dollar fine!"

The judge's own temper broke out of its flimsy harness. "That's my prerogative!" he snapped. "You run the streets . . . I'll run the courts."

Buford pointed a finger. "If I bring them in, and you let them go, the whole thing becomes a big joke . . . and I don't care to trade lives for laughs. From now on I want *maximum* penalties."

The judge's face turned crimson. He reached for the huge *Criminal Code Book* on the book shelf behind him, and slammed the volume on the desk. "*You* want . . . *you* want! Why you self-appointed dictator, all you know is force and violence! You don't understand the simplest precepts of law!"

"I know the difference between a poor honest judge, and a rich *dishonest* one." He lifted the heavy volume. "And by tomorrow morning, I'll learn what's in this *Criminal Code Book* . . . word for word." He slid off the edge of the desk and moved toward the door. "What you've got to worry about, *your honor*, is what part of it I can use against you."

Buford tossed a salute and departed.

In the morning, when Buford appeared at the courthouse at an early hour, he had a definite purpose. There was much work to be done before the judge started his professional day. He rounded up the janitors, and just about everyone else who wasn't committed to some other function. He set them into rapid motion.

An hour later, the janitors were wheeling their final carts filled with law books. Buford awaited them outside the door of the basement men's room. "Is that everything?" Buford asked.

They assured him it was. Buford looked at his watch. The timing had been perfect. It was exactly 8:59. If the judge was as much a creature of habit as Buford believed, he would be arriving in just about one minute. Buford watched the seconds tick off. When thirty had passed, a loud voice could be heard echoing through the subterranean labyrinth.

"What the hell's going on here!"

Buford leaned against the wall, and when Judge Clarke charged out of the stairwell, Buford unfolded his arm in a grand flourish, pointing to the men's room door.

"What?" the Judge questioned, almost running in circles. "What is this . . . tell me?"

"Please, Judge," Buford coaxed. "Step inside."

The judge snorted, looking about, but finally did as he was asked. He entered the men's room and let out an immediate wail of fury. He saw his desk and chair in the middle of the room, with his library lining the tiled wall. A small leather-topped table with a weather vane lamp was nestled between the two urinals. Buford smiled benignly, hugging the *Criminal Code Book* to his chest.

"We hope you'll like it, Judge," Buford said sweetly. "Of course, there's no telephone yet . . . but you won't need one today."

With his fist doubled, almost apoplectic, the judge raged: "I demand to know the meaning of this outrage. . . . How dare you!"

"Oh," said Buford, with an expression of little-boy innocence. "I read the book, your honor. It clearly states, page fifty-three, paragraph six, that the sheriff has the right to assign courtrooms and judge's chambers. In view of your past judgments, I thought you might feel more at home here." The judge's chest was heaving in breathless exasperation. He looked from Buford to the urinals, to the toilets. "There's a list," Buford went on, "of search and arrest warrants I want made out by three o'clock. I'll have your lunch sent in . . . two crow sandwiches and a glass of pride." He started away, but paused. "Oh . . . if one word about these warrants—you'll excuse the expression— *leaks* out . . . your distinguished career is over . . . page ninety-two, section four."

Buford moved to the urinals and gently placed the volume on the table between them. He sniffed, wrinkled his nose, gave his head a shake that said, "sorry about that," and left. The judge was too flabbergasted to speak.

By late afternoon all deputies were on hand at Buford's farm. Buford passed out the warrants—which the judge had obediently processed—while Pauline served cold beers. Buford's father was also present for the briefing —and the refreshments. When everybody had a drink and a warrant, Buford picked up his big stick and paced before them.

"The preliminaries are over, men," he said firmly. "We know each other, and we know the size of the problem. I was elected sheriff on one issue . . . that I'd clean up every joint in the county. We're going to start doing that tomorrow. First, I don't want any car, truck, or driver that even looks like a moonshiner to move on the roads. Lonnie, you and Chris cover Highways Forty-five and Sixty-four." They nodded in agreement. "The State Highway Patrol will take over our normal traffic duties. I hear there are four new stills operating: two near Big Mill Road, one over in Donald Springs, and one back up in Pepper Hill. Grady, that's your department. . . . Knock 'em flat."

Grady looked around. "Alone?"

Buford turned to his father.

"Me and six loggers might just happen to be around when you look over your shoulder," he said.

"The rest of us," Buford said, "will wait until the illegal liquor is flowing, the girls are making their trailer runs, and the suckers are crowding the tables. That's when we hit . . . fast and hard. Arrest the owners, let the girls and the customers go . . . bust every joint. Obra, you're in charge of the east half. . . ." Obra nodded. "And Virgil," he said to the red-necked deputy of about Buford's size, "you run the west half."

"Big job," said the deputy with a frown.

"You're a big man," Buford said. "This whole operation rests on one thing . . . surprise."

Some of the men had questions after the orientation, but most drove off with their orders. Virgil Button drove directly home, changed clothes, and drove his pickup truck to the Green Lantern Bar. A few minutes later, he was outlining the details of the raids to a highly receptive audience. In the huddle with Virgil at the far end of the bar were Callie, Augie and Jaggers. Luan Paxton and Margie Ann were in a booth with two men. The curious meeting at the bar arrested Luan's attention.

Buford was keyed up for the kill, and his palms were sweaty the next afternoon when he took the microphone in his hand. He watched the second hand on his watch, and when it was right, he said: "This is five-oh-one to all units . . . *now!*"

102

During the entire afternoon the story was much the same. When Lonnie ripped a tarp off a pickup truck, he found a load of watermelons instead of moonshine; Obra burst into Lockman's Bar with gun drawn, but found everyone holding a toast to him. The beverage was milk; when another deputy yanked open a trailer door he found himself staring at an old lady who was deeply absorbed in her knitting. The biggest laugh of all came at the Lucky Spot. When deputies charged into the gaming room they intruded on a spirited ping-pong game complete with cheering spectators.

At a crossroads rendezvous point, Buford sat in his cruiser with Grady. Grady had parked across the street. After a long silence, Buford slammed his fist against the steering wheel.

"They knew! They all *knew!* Somebody tipped them off!"

"We can try again tomorrow night," said Grady, as disconsolate as his boss.

"No! Not till we find out who and why."

"The why," Grady said, "is simple . . . money."

Buford clenched a massive fist. "If I find him . . . he won't live to spend it!" He exhaled in a gush, then said wearily: "Good night, Grady . . . I'm going home."

Grady said good-night as he got out. The moment the door was closed Buford renewed his anger. He squealed the cruiser off into the night.

He traveled the country road faster than he should, but his fermenting anger demanded speed. Even at his excessive speed—more than seventy—he was doubly surprised to see a car

103

drawing toward him in the rearview mirror. He gasped in disbelief when the car very nearly rammed his back, but then it swerved past him. In the momentary glimpse into the passing car, Buford saw a girl with long blonde hair. She was alone, and was defying him. Her car then cut in front of him almost locking with his front bumper. "You caught me in the wrong mood, lady," Buford said aloud, gritting his teeth. He floored the gas pedal and took chase.

With his flasher spinning, and his siren wailing, Buford hit speeds in excess of one hundred miles an hour, but on a lonely stretch of wooded road he finally convinced the driver to pull over.

Buford parked on the shoulder behind the yellow convertible, and rushed to the door. "Just what kind of a game do you think you're playing?" he said, leaning over.

He saw a pleasant smile on a pretty face, and a millisecond later he saw more, but too late. A pair of forty-five caliber automatics poked out of the back seat and fired. Bullets struck Buford in the face and shoulder, driving him across the highway. Rapidly, the guns fired additional rounds as the car geared up and sped away.

Sprawled on his back, forming a cross with his arms, Buford bled. One hole, ringed with powder burns, marked his cheek. Several wounds were scattered over his chest. Not a muscle moved in his massive body. Blood began to gurgle from the wounds onto the highway.

Chapter Eleven

"On The Take" . . . And On the Mend

Pauline had been worried all evening, but when Buford failed to call by midnight, she checked with the Sheriff's Department. The dispatcher told her that everyone had either checked in personally or had called in and gone home for the night. With her intuition nagging at her, she called Grady. He reassured her and promised he would raise Buford on his radio.

A half hour later, Pauline heard the sound of a car in the driveway and ran to the porch. "Buford's home . . . he's safe!" she said aloud, at the sight of the headlights. But her hopes plummeted. She saw Grady get out of the car.

"We haven't been able to get through to him," he said. "Can't figure it out. He was going straight home."

"Have they checked Route Twenty-two? Sometimes Buford comes home that way."

"I'll double back," said Grady.

"I'm coming with you," Pauline said, already moving toward the door.

The blue flasher light of Grady's cruiser sent eerie patterns over the country landscape; his headlights were on high beam. They rounded a tight curve, and Grady had to hit the brakes hard. Just ahead, Buford's black cruiser could be seen parked along the shoulder.

"That's it!" Pauline cried out. "That's his car."

Grady was silent, realizing something was very wrong. Then as he drew behind the abandoned black car, they simultaneously caught sight of the sprawled figure in the opposite traffic lane.

"Oh, no . . . NO!" Pauline got out of the car before Grady made a complete stop. She ran to the blood-saturated figure. "Buford!"

Grady ran to catch up, as Pauline dropped to her knees. She cradled Buford's head and was bordering on hysteria at the sight of his blood. "Darling, darling. . . !"

Buford's eyes opened slowly. "Hi . . . honey."

"Thank God!" she cried, using her hand to wipe some of the blood from his face.

Grady took a look, and bolted for his cruiser. He reached inside to grab the mike. "Get me an ambulance out on Highway Twenty-two near the Carlson place," he demanded. "And *hurry!*"

When Grady returned to Buford's side, he saw blood trickling from his mouth. He attempted to assess the damage, but there was no way. The best reassurance came with Buford's rational speech.

"Stop crying, sweetheart," Buford said clearly. "I'm okay. Just . . . resting, that's all."

The dresser in Buford's bedroom had been cleared. On it was a towel with an array of medical instruments. On the floor was a growing pile of bloody bandages and pads. Pauline assisted Dr. Stivers as he finished bandaging Buford's head. He was bound from chest to head, with only his eyes, mouth, and nose still exposed. The doctor filled a syringe and Buford slowly opened his eyes.

"What's . . . that for?" he mumbled.

The doctor smiled. "Something to make you relax . . . to help you get your strength back."

Buford shook his head determinedly. "I . . . don't want to relax."

The doctor would have his way this time. He jabbed the hypodermic needle into Buford's upper arm. "You're going to," he said, "and while you're doing it, try to think of a new profession. You're not very good at this one."

The sedative was a powerful one, and its effects were almost instantaneous. "I'm learning, Doc, I'm learning. Made the . . . mistake of . . . trying to fight . . . clean. When . . . when I get up . . . I'm going to . . . to drop kick them . . . right in the . . . right in the. . . ."

Buford was asleep.

The living room was alive with potted plants and floral arrangements. A table was piled high with get-well cards. There was a huge box of expensive chocolates, bottles of Jack Daniels whiskey, and a large canister of tubed cigars. Grady stood by while Buford spoke on the telephone. Between phrases, he alternated between sips of a tall bourbon drink, and puffs of a long black cigar.

"Yes . . . well thank you very much," he concluded. "I appreciate that. All right . . . goodbye."

He hung up the telephone and adjusted the blanket on his lap. He stretched out on the chaise longue as a man of leisure. His face and neck were still bandaged, but if he bore pain it was not apparent. Pauline entered the room behind him, as Buford puffed again at his cigar. He

107

looked at it for a moment, and used it to point at the seemingly embarrassed Grady Coker.

"A man doesn't know how many friends he has," said Buford, "until he's flat on his back."

"Or, how many people are glad he is," said Grady.

Buford gestured toward the table. "Look at the pile of cards. Why, there's even one from Augie McCullah." He laughed. "Didn't even know he could write. Chocolates from the bar girls, dollar cigars from Willie Rae, Tennessee sippin' whiskey from Callie, a pair of loaded dice from the Lucky Spot—that roll sevens every time—and *flowers*. See that big wreath? All the way from Nashville. Mr. Witter, no less. Grab a handful of cigars, Grady . . . and a couple of bottles. Pauline, would you build Grady a highball?"

"No thanks," said Grady. "I don't want anything."

"Why not?" Buford asked. "It's the fruit of our labor. Afraid you'll be corrupted . . . *again?*"

Pauline moved in quickly. "Buford! That wasn't a nice thing to say."

Grady's eyes narrowed. "Are you going on the take, Buford?"

"I sure am," he said with a grin.

Grady drew in a deep breath. "In that case. . . ." He started to unpin his badge.

"Yes, sir, Grady. I'm going to take and take and *take* until they've got nothing left to give but their *blood!*" Buford's voice broke with anger. He threw his cigar across the room, and knocked his highball off the table. It crashed on the floor.

"Buford!" Pauline gasped in alarm.

"Then," Buford went on, "I'm going to take that blood from them . . . one drop at a time!"

"Buford . . . darling . . . please don't," Pauline begged.

Buford pushed Pauline's hand aside, as Grady refastened his badge. "I'm going to start, Grady . . . with the informer."

"Do you know who he is?" Grady asked.

"A little bird just called me on the phone," he said, ". . . and I'm going after him with my bare hands! We'd have closed the county in one night if he hadn't. . . ." Buford was exhausted. He slumped back on the chaise, breathing heavily. He grimaced with pain. "You know," he said laughing wryly, "he was the only one who didn't send me a get-well card."

Pauline followed Grady outside after he finished the meeting with Buford. When they were down the steps, she said: "I don't know what to do, Grady. He's been like that ever since the shooting. Smoking their cigars, drinking their whiskey and smelling their flowers. I guess that's to remind himself how much he hates them. Then he gets all worked up into a rage."

"I guess he's earned that right," Grady said.

"But it's gone beyond all reason. It's a kind of madness."

Grady paused beside his cruiser, and took his gun from its holster. "Maybe that's what it will take to clean out that snake pit." He extended the gun toward Pauline. "And . . . this."

She shook her head, and turned away. "No."

"You heard him, Pauline," said Grady, passionately. "He said 'bare hands.' Bare hands are no match against guns."

"Grady," Pauline said, weakly. "You know how I feel about . . . them."

"And so does Buford. He won't put one on unless you let him. So you've got to decide which you want to spend your old age with . . . fear . . . or your husband."

Pauline drew a hand to her face and studied the weapon thoughtfully.

When Pauline returned to the living room, Buford was asleep. She went to an upstairs closet, and reached on the shelf among stored linens. Her hand touched leather and she took it into her hands. She stared at the belt and holster and at the blue steel revolver it contained. Slowly, with the gun belt held away from her body, she returned downstairs. Gently, so as not to waken Buford, she placed the object of fear and hate on his lap. She paused, staring at her handiwork for a long troubled moment. With a feeling of bewildered sorrow, she turned and left the room.

Chapter Twelve

Back to the War

It wasn't a medical decision: it was Buford's. When he determined he was ready to return to the job, he did so. That morning he dressed in one of his casual sport shirts that had become as much a work trademark as his big stick, pulled on a pair of casual slacks and a pair of leather boots. He went down to breakfast, and although he wasn't dressed much differently than he had during his weeks of convalescence, Pauline knew his intentions.

"Something tells me you've decided you're well enough to get back on the job," she said, as she served hot cakes.

He grinned. "Sometimes I think you're a mind reader. But it's true."

"You know what the doctor said. He said you shouldn't try to. . . ."

Buford held up a hand. "I owe Doc plenty," he said. "I may owe him my very life, but he's still a doctor, and doctors have a role they have to play. He's playing his role, and I'm playing mine."

"Are you sure you're ready, Buford?"

He nodded. "I'm sure."

In deference to Pauline, Buford didn't wear the gun belt when he left the house, but he strapped it on before he faced his deputies an hour later down near the highway. The gun was in place but the big stick was in his hand also. It had become a habit. He paced in front of the men in deep thought. He was aware of their curiosity about his wounds; the red, ugly one on his face was obvious, but he didn't refer to it, and neither did any of them.

"We've all had a nice long vacation with pay," he began finally. There was a ripple of constrained laughter. "And now it's back to the war. We're going to take up exactly where we left off . . . only this time we're not going to separate. We're going to hit them as a team . . . everywhere . . . in force. Any questions?"

Virgil Button broke from the ranks, and nervously looked around. "I'd like to call home," he said. "To let 'em know I'll be late."

Buford was shaking his head "no" before the phrase was completed. "*No* calls . . . *no* radio communications . . . and *nobody* out of my sight. Okay . . . we'll start with the stills." He turned and started toward his car. "Follow me."

The first raid caught a large moonshine operation unawares. A dozen workers were herded into patrol cars, and bottled whiskey and mash barrels were put into the center of the clearing along with the still. Dynamite charges were wired to eliminate the operation once and for all.

Inspecting the wiring, Buford said, "Virgil, I don't like the way these dynamite charges are wired. Just don't look quite right to me."

"I don't see nothin' wrong with them," Virgil said, taking a closer look.

"Well you're new at this," said Buford. "Let's check them."

Buford started toward the mound of contraband materials. Virgil shrugged and followed. Buford traced a wire to a dynamite plant, and leaned over to check it out. Virgil

112

checked another charge a few feet away. Buford tapped Virgil on the shoulder. The expression on Virgil's face was clearly one of annoyance, and this suited Buford perfectly. Before Virgil could mouth a remark, Buford slammed a fist into the deputy's mouth. He sprawled flat on his back.

"Why you son of a bitch!" Virgil mumbled, as he got to his knees. For a moment Virgil licked at the blood inside his lip. Then he lunged toward Buford. "You want a fight, you'll get. . . ."

Buford stepped aside. He drove a fist to the back of Vigil's neck, sending him face down into the dust. If nothing else, Buford could admire the informer's staying power. He was no coward. Cursing under his breath, and spitting blood, Virgil got to his feet. His arms were spread wide as he stalked his attacker. Buford deliberately dropped his guard and pretended to move off. In his perimeter vision, Buford saw the wild right fist coming his way. He ducked, grabbed the arm and flipped his willing adversary in a flailing somersault. Now Buford followed him. When Virgil moved once more to his feet, Buford ended the battle with another vicious fist to the jaw. Virgil hit the ground, managed to crawl to his knees, but knelt there dazedly, as though silently begging for pity.

With his nostrils still flared in anger, Buford strode back to the detonator. The other deputies had gathered there to watch the fight. Buford grabbed the handle of the detonator as if to blow everything, including Virgil, into oblivion.

"My God!" Obra exclaimed in disbelief.

"Buford . . . don't!" yelled Grady.

Grady and Obra lunged for Buford and grabbed his arms. In a violent flurry of resistance, Buford freed himself and sent both deputies to the ground. "Get away! I know what I'm doing!"

He knew he was looking like a madman, but he didn't care what anyone thought. He had rehearsed this action too long in his mind to be put off. The other deputies moved back to a safe distance, and Buford once more grabbed the detonator handle. By this time, Virgil had become sentient enough to realize what was taking place. Seeing Buford grab the handle the second time, he looked around in terror, trying to find a place to run.

"Don't run, Virgil!" Buford shouted. "You'll never make it!"

"Buford . . . Buford!" Virgil cried out. "For God's sake . . . don't. Please don't!"

Buford knelt before the detonator, the handle held firmly in his grip. "Tell 'em, Virgil . . . tell everybody who tipped them off. Tell 'em how they knew I took the back way home at night!"

Virgil's mouth moved, but words failed.

Buford made a move, as though to plunge the handle. *"Tell them!"*

Virgil staggered on his feet, gesturing pitifully. "It . . . it was me, but you see . . . they. . . ."

"Down on your knees! Down!"

Grady spoke from the side. "Buford . . . it's cold-blooded murder. You can't. . . ."

Buford ignored the plea. "Now crawl. Crawl over here to me. Come on, Virgil . . . *crawl!*"

Virgil began to crawl. He was whimpering, certain he would die.

"Crawl faster . . . *faster!* You haven't got much time!"

In the realization there was a faint glimmer of hope, Virgil began to creep furiously, frantically . . . as though propelled by an engine.

"Faster . . . faster!" Buford yelled, taking perverse pleasure in the spectacle.

When the moment was right, Buford gave the detonator a violent plunge downward. The explosion was deafening, with dust, rocks and wood splinters spraying over the countryside. The still, mash barrels, and liquor were quickly enveloped in flame and smoke. The deputies took instant cover, but Buford held ground. He knew he was safely out of range, and was equally certain that Virgil was low enough to the ground to escape injury. Before the reverberations had died down, Buford went to the sniveling deputy who remained on hands and knees.

"Stand up!" Buford demanded.

Virgil stumbled and fell to the ground on his first attempt to rise. Finally he managed to right himself on wobbly legs.

Buford reached out and ripped the deputy badge from Virgil's shirt pocket, taking pocket and all. "Walk home," he said.

Virgil sniffled and lowered his head. He turned to begin his humiliating, ten-mile hike.

The day's activities were as successful as the earlier raids had been disastrous. A second still was destroyed and the operators arrested. Buford commandeered a school bus and directed the driver to follow the procession of police vehicles. With swiftness and total lack of resistance the striking force cleaned out three dens of vice, including Lockman's Bar. By the time the bus rolled to a halt in front of the Green Lantern, it was three-quarters filled with professional women of all ages and colors.

The deputies cleaned out the trailers at the Green Lantern without arousing the attention of the staff members inside. One customer was sent scurrying out of a trailer with trousers in hand. Buford emerged moments later with the still-naked hustler, who angrily attempted to get into a robe as she was being marched toward the bus. Buford gave her a slap on the behind to quicken her pace. With a deputy left behind as a guard, Buford led the others inside. The bar was crowded with girls and customers. It was so busy that Prentiss had a second bartender at work with him behind the bar.

All activity halted with the entrance of the Sheriff's Department, but the blaring jukebox continued its country and western offering. Buford pointed to a girl at the bar. "Pick her up," he said to a deputy. He walked past several customers to another girl. "Her, too."

Grady approached the girl. "You're under arrest," he told her.

Her male companion, half-drunk, turned to Grady. "Now just a damn minute!"

"You want to come, too?" Grady asked. He scurried away promptly.

Buford pointed out a pair of girls in a booth, labeling them for arrest, and looked at Prentiss Parley. Prentiss was standing at the end of the bar, next to Zoltan Dicks. They didn't seem happy. Just as Buford was wondering where

Callie was, she came charging in from her rear living quarters.

"What the hell's going on here?" she demanded.

Buford went to her, and took her by the arm. "Let's go for a walk," he said, leading her behind the bar.

Zoltan Dicks made the mistake of interceding. "Take your hands off. . . ."

Buford gave him a backhand to the face that sent him sprawling like a rag doll. With the same movement, Buford gave Callie a shove toward the storeroom door.

"All right, Callie," he said, "you've got the key. Open it up."

She faced him defiantly. "You got a warrant?"

"Yeah," he said, lifting a foot. He smashed the sole of his boot against the door, and it splintered from its hinges. "I keep it in my shoe."

The room was stacked high with illegal whiskey.

The raids prompted another meeting of underworld, which took place the next morning at the Green Lantern. The chairs were stacked on the tables, and the door was locked to early bar traffic. Clustered about the corner of the bar were Callie, Jaggers, Otie Doss, Augie, Prentiss, and several subordinate hoods including Zoltan Dicks.

"He knew exactly where everything was, and when to hit it," Callie said in disgust. "I tell you he's got someone down here, working on the inside."

117

"Not from my group," said Jaggers. "My people are solid."

"Oh, your people are real solid," Callie said, sarcastically, "like that bunch you sent for from Alabama. Couldn't put him away when they were two feet away from him. That really started something."

"How much help have you and Prentiss been?" said Augie McCullah. "Those tramps and that pimp of yours have been robbing everybody that passes through town."

Prentiss bristled. "Get off it, Augie!"

"You run your store," said Callie, "and I'll run mine." After a brief pause: "I talked to Witter this morning. He said to put him away. Believe me, I'll take care of that son of a bitch. Don't give a damn what it costs."

"I've been operating in this county for twenty years," said Augie. "Get this straight . . . you're not running my show. If I want to do any killing, I'll do it without a board meeting. Count me out." Augie was off his stool before finishing his remark. He turned and left the bar.

Zoltan Dicks looked at Callie. "Why do you want to bring in outsiders to do a job I've done a half-dozen times?"

"Sure," said Prentiss. "You also did four years for the last one."

Zoltan grinned. "But the guy's still dead."

All eyes studied Zoltan in silent consideration.

It had been a painful and bitter struggle, but at last Buford felt as though he had gained control of his county. He and his men were knocking off the gambling operators with regularity, and even Judge Clarke had begun to show some semblance of cooperation. With matters running so smoothly, Buford started to spend much more time with his neglected family. He turned night operations over to Grady Coker so he could even regain some interest in television.

After enjoying a meal of pot roast and mashed potatoes, Buford joined his family in the living room. This would be his third straight night of televiewing, hopefully without interruption. The children tuned in a detective program and lay on the floor to watch it. A single lamp was lit on the table in the picture window. Buford sat on the couch beside Pauline, and held hands with her as though they were courting. His bone-handled magnum revolver lay in its belt and holster on an end table. When he placed it there before dinner, he had been sure it would not be needed for the rest of the day.

The television action had just begun again after the first commercial. Then it happened. The room exploded in a deafening blast of terror. The window shattered under the impact, spewing glass across the room. The lamp fell to the floor and crashed. Blast after blast sprayed the room.

Buford thrust Pauline to the floor. "Lie flat kids . . . lie flat!" He scrambled on his knees to the end table. As he found his gun, he saw the blasts coming from beside a tree outside the window. Shep was barking crazily, clawing to get out the front door.

Buford, in stocking feet, ran to the door and flung it open. In a single leap he was off the porch and running. He edged around the side of the house with gun poised and ready.

He leaned around the corner to see Zoltan Dicks pump another round into a shotgun. It was night, but there was moonlight enough to identify the gun bearer clearly. Buford came around the house, firing. Shep was already charging. The dog was mid-air in a ferocious leap when the shotgun caught him. He flipped in a circle and fell to the ground.

As Zoltan ducked behind the tree, Buford's slug ripped bark where Zoltan had been. He ran after the figure that had now started running toward the catfish pond. At the edge of the pond Zoltan turned to fire once more. The blast didn't get off. Buford had already knelt to take careful aim. He fired. The magnum shell tore into Zoltan's body, twisting him in one direction and then another. With the third blast, the shotgun fell aside, and Zoltan fell backwards into the pond. Buford emptied his gun, to make very sure. Then, breathing heavily, with anger and sorrow bringing tears to his eyes, Buford returned to find Shep.

Pauline was crouched in a darkened corner of the room clinging to Dwana. Mike lay on the floor nearby. They watched the open front door in terrified silence. They heard the boards creak on the steps, and saw a huge figure filling the doorway. "It's dad," Mike cried out. He went to a lamp and lit it.

There was a moment of silence as they faced him. Buford, still with gun in hand, carried the German shepherd into the house. Tears streamed down his cheeks.

"Shep's dead," Dwana cried out. "They killed Shep!"

She tried to reach out to touch the bleeding animal, but her mother restrained her. Words at this time were meaningless. Every family member cried in bitter despair.

Chapter Thirteen

" 'Twas The Week Before Christmas . . ."

Buford knew there would be little chance of proving a conspiracy involving Zoltan Dicks and the local operators. They insisted they had no knowledge of Zoltan's murder attempt against Buford but said he had been drinking heavily on the night of the shooting. The matter was turned over to the grand jury for investigation, however, and Buford considered this a step in the right direction. Six months earlier, a grand jury would not have been called. Judge Clarke hadn't exactly become a friend, but he *was* running scared, and that was what Buford wanted.

Several days after the shooting, Buford had been in the hills tracking down moonshiners. He returned late to find a cryptic message awaiting him at headquarters. He understood it at once. It said: "Call on the hour. Important." It was signed: "L. Lookfree."

Buford hurried to the nearest phone booth, since the hour had just passed, and frantically dialed the phone booth number at the Green Lantern. He sighed with relief at the sound of a feminine voice. "That you, Lookfree," he said, using the code name. It came from their first encounter when he had found her bosom so interesting.

"I've been trying to reach you for more than an hour," she said, excitedly. "Prentiss has Margie Ann in Callie's trailer. They think she's your informer, because they found out she used

122

to be Grady's playmate. It's awful . . . you better get to her in a hurry." She hung up; Buford was on his way.

Buford was careful not to arouse unnecessary attention as he sped to the Strip. He neither sounded his siren nor used his flasher light. But he did speed. He arrived within five minutes after Luan's call, and parked under a grove of trees at the edge of the Green Lantern trailer lot. He ran between the trailers until he came to the one parked directly adjacent to the back door of the bar. He tried three windows before he could see inside, but on the fourth try he was successful. It was a high window, but he was a tall man.

He saw Prentiss and another hood working over the shapely young girl. Prentiss strapped her with a belt and buckle as the other held her face against the mattress. Margie Ann, totally naked, was covered with bloody welts. In his submiliminal view, Buford could also see Callie sitting in the corner at a table. A bottle of whiskey was before her, half-emptied.

Buford had no idea how securely the door might be locked, but it didn't matter. He was coming in. He took a few steps back and surged forward with all his energy. His shoulder sent the door swinging inward with a metalic clunk. "No one moves," he said. His magnum was drawn.

In the tableau, he saw terror on three faces. Callie blinked, open-mouthed. Prentiss was sweating profusely from his vigorous workout, but his face suddenly drained of color. The other man, a heavyset burly character Buford had never seen before, seemed to be trying to melt into the trailer paneling. Blood was everywhere, on the sheets, the floor, and the walls. Margie Ann appeared to be about one belt buckle blow away from death.

Buford went to her and turned her face to the side. Both eyes were blackened and swollen shut, her lips were bloody and swollen to double size. She tried to speak, but only gasps came from her battered mouth. There wasn't an inch of her naked body that had escaped fists or the belt.

Buford looked up at Prentiss, who was wild-eyed with fear. With a sweep of his forearm, Buford smashed Prentiss against the wall. His head struck the paneling and he slumped to the floor. Buford turned to the other thug, who was trapped in the corner of the room. Buford beckoned him with a bent forefinger. When the man ventured closer, Buford whipped him across his face with the pistol. He fell into the corner, unconscious. Buford started to turn toward Callie, and was glad he did. She was reaching for the whiskey bottle, but that wasn't what endangered him. He turned in time to see another of Callie's hoods entering the trailer, and he was carrying a shotgun. Buford kicked the gun free, tripping the man, and kicked him viciously in the groin.

"Go ahead, Callie, throw it. . . ." Buford said, aiming his gun at her. "All I want is an excuse!" Callie let the bottle drop from her hand.

Buford picked up a sheet from the floor, and tossed it over Margie Ann. He moved beyond the bed to where Prentiss had been deposited.

He yanked him to his feet and slammed him against the wall.

Holding him at arm's length, he said: "You're entitled to a phone call." Prentiss stared at him half-consciously, his eyes blinking. Buford drove a hard right fist into his face.

"You hear me, fella," Buford said. "You're entitled to one phone call." Buford kneed him in the groin.

"You . . . don't have to make a statement without advice of counsel!" Buford kneed him again, and when he bent over, he slammed his head against the wall.

"You're under arrest for white slavery, for assault and battery, for kidnapping, torture, for everything I can find in the book!"

Buford yanked Prentiss to his feet and spun him around. He drove his foot into his behind, sending him sprawling through the door and onto the ground outside. Buford hoisted the latest arrival from the floor—where he had remained since he was kicked in the groin—and sent him flying out the door after Prentiss. The third man, who had been floored by Buford's pistol, was still unconscious. Buford thrust a hand under his belt and dragged him to the door. He booted him into the pile with the others.

A few days later, Buford drove his cruiser along a rural highway. After a few miles he pulled off and followed a service road into a glen. He stopped the car and looked at his passenger. It was the same girl he had encountered that first day at the Lucky Spot—but there had been changes. For one thing, she wore no see-through blouse, and had only minimal makeup on her young, attractive face. On the back seat rested a pair of large suitcases.

"It's payday, Luan," he said, smiling. As she lighted a cigarette, Buford pulled a folded legal document from his pocket. He tossed it into her lap. "A present from me to you . . . warrants and charges against you have been taken off the books."

Luan stared at the papers in her lap.

"I don't know why you risked your life helping me," he said, "but I appreciate it."

She drew from her cigarette, stared at him a moment, then smiled. "I've got a soft spot for big good-looking Marine-types," she said. "My husband was a Marine, but he didn't make it through Vietnam."

Buford frowned. "I didn't know that . . . I'm sorry. But you've got plenty of time ahead of you. You've got to get as far away from this place as you can. Start a new life for yourself . . . not *this* kind of life."

She nodded and fingered the document on her lap. "Margie Ann wants to meet me somewhere when she's well enough," she said. "We'd like to get into something else . . . but how? With what?"

Buford had a roll of bills concealed in his hand. He poked it neatly into her dress, between her breasts. "Special funds account," he said.

She smiled. "From your piggy bank?"

"From the crap table at the Lucky Spot. Wish I could do more."

"So do I . . . but then, you wouldn't be the kind of man you are . . . would you?"

Luan leaned over and kissed Buford full on

126

the lips. He caught his breath, looked at her a moment, and started the car.

"I'll see you safely to the bus depot," he said.

It was the shortest fall in Buford's memory, and suddenly the Christmas holiday season had arrived. Aside from his family's well-being, his greatest Christmas wish would have been a quick conviction of Callie Hacker and her thugs, and the shutting down of Jaggers' place and the others. It hadn't come to that. Callie was out on bail, awaiting trial, and Prentiss was being held without bond. The Green Lantern was still operating, as was the Lucky Spot, but nothing like in the past. If there was gambling going on, it was done on the quiet, and only with trusted customers. His several-month career as sheriff had brought some positive changes, at least. For this, he was grateful.

After a hectic day of last-minute Christmas shopping, Buford returned home with a car full of packages. He entered the house to find the entire family engaged in the trimming of a huge Christmas tree. Dwana and Mike were stringing popcorn and cranberries from two large bowls on the floor. Pauline was helping Grandma and Grandpa place their carefully wrapped presents under the tree.

"Ho, ho, ho," Buford said, as he lowered his presents on the couch. "I come bearing gifts."

Pauline greeted him with a kiss and a hug. "Thank goodness you're home," she said joyfully. "Now we can begin the best Christmas Eve we've ever had."

Mike was already handling the long box Buford had just deposited. It was no secret, after

127

lifting it, that his dream of owning a shotgun would at last be realized.

"Put it down, Michael," said his mother.

"Gee . . . wonder what it is?" Mike said innocently.

"Yes, I wonder," Pauline said with a wince.

"Say, you know something?" said Grandpa. "This is quite an occasion. First time the family's been together like this in, lo, these many years. I would say. . . ."

Grandma, Pauline and Buford joined him in unison: "This calls for a drink."

Buford reached down to the couch for a special package. When the laughter died down, he said: "Pauline, wonder if you'd go to the kitchen and get us some glasses. Just happens I remembered to pick up a nice bottle of Tennessee sippin' whiskey."

"None for me, you know that, Buford," said Grandma. "But before you men folk get all wobbly-kneed with Christmas cheer, there are still some packages in the car. Son, would you get the turkey and pies, and be careful to keep the turkey covered."

Buford winked at Pauline. "Yes, mother," he said as the obedient son.

"And Dwana," Grandma said. "There's something for you . . . I left it in the kitchen."

"For me?" she said, dropping a handful of popcorn back into the bowl. She ran to the kitchen, and Buford lingered at the door to watch. In a moment Dwana appeared in the kitchen door, holding a basket. The blanket had been turned back, and through the opening appeared the small black and brown head of a German shepherd puppy. Tears were in

128

Dwana's eyes, and her emotion was contagious. "This is the nicest gift I ever got . . . a puppy. Oh, thanks, Grandma. Thank you very much!"

A few miles away there was another celebration taking place, but all the participants weren't enjoying it. The Christmas Eve party at the Green Lantern had become a tradition, and Callie could think of no convenient excuse to cancel it. So, as the tree was being trimmed, and as free drinks were being poured, she sat at her favorite corner of the bar, getting drunk. Several of the girls brought presents to put under the tree, and others were busy hanging bunting and streamers.

Amid the festive activity, a jewelry salesman named Sheldon Levine took a few watches from a jewelry case he had rested on the bar. It was never too late to do a little extra Christmas business. He showed the wares to one of the bar girls, who gave it a cursory glance, but returned to the more exciting activity beneath the mistletoe.

He moved downward along the bar to Callie. "Merry Christmas, Callie," he said amiably. He placed two watches and a bracelet on the bar in front of her. "These were made for a woman like you, Callie . . . elegance . . . taste."

Callie shoved the jewelry aside, and motioned for the bartender. "Haven't you heard, Sheldon?" she said, thick-tongued. "We're in a depression."

He held a combination watch-bracelet in front of her. "Everyone needs a good watch."

"All it's good for is to remind me I'm sitting here on my ass losing money every time it ticks." She took a long swallow of the drink the bar-

129

tender poured. "And I'm getting Goddamned mad about it!" She drained the glass and threw it on the floor.

Sheldon knew a cue when he received one. He turned and scurried to a booth where better moods prevailed.

When he was occupied with a sales pitch to one of the girls, Callie called the bartender over. She whispered into his ear. He nodded, and left the bar. Outside, he examined a ring of master keys, and selected one. He went to a black, late model Cadillac, and after several attempts, turned the proper key in the trunk lock. The lid sprung open. He lifted the heavy jewelry cases from it, and carried them to the back door of the bar.

Buford and Grandpa were into their second Christmas Eve toddy when the phone rang. Since Pauline was busy in the kitchen with Grandma, Buford answered it. It was Grady.

"I've got a Mr. Levine down here, Sheriff," Grady said. "Claims some sixty thousand dollars worth of jewelry was hoisted from the trunk of his car . . . over at the Green Lantern."

Buford looked over his shoulder at the happy scene in the living room. "Probably stole it himself," he said. Then, with a sigh of resignation: "Okay . . . I'll be there in a few minutes."

Pauline entered the living room from the kitchen as Buford was strapping on his gun belt.

"Don't open the presents till I get back," he said.

"Buford," Pauline said with disappointment. "Not on Christmas Eve."

"It's just a burglary. Won't take long."

130

While Buford studied the report at the station, Callie was making special preparations for the climax to the Green Lantern Christmas party. In her office, she examined a sawed-off shotgun. She reached into a drawer full of shells and expertly loaded it. She stepped over the stolen jewelry cases to the safe where she took the 38-caliber revolver off a shelf. She checked the chamber, and found it was fully loaded. She emptied her purse on her desk, and placed the revolver inside it. Then, careful to cover the shotgun with a fur stole, she put it under her arm, picked up her purse and reentered the bar.

As she took her place at the end of the bar, a newly arrived bar girl waved at her. "Merry Christmas, Callie," she called.

Callie waved drunkenly. "Santa Claus is on his way," she slurred. "Jingle balls . . . and I do mean *balls*." She was in position facing the door, her weapons ready for Santa Claus's arrival.

A few minutes later, Buford drew his cruiser to a stop at the front door of the Green Lantern. Levine was beside him in the front seat. A moment later, Grady's car came to a stop next to them. The three got out of the cars and went to the bar entrance. The strains of "Rudolph The Red-Nosed Raindeer" could be heard from inside.

They entered the bar to find the party in full swing. Because of the throng of freeloaders and the smoke, Buford didn't see Callie on her throne at the end of the bar—not until she opened fire: "WHAM!"

The blast was centered at the door, inches from where Buford had entered. In reflex,

Buford ducked, but in doing so he shoved Levine under the Christmas tree. He also pushed Grady to the floor on his opposite side. Buford drew his gun and dove for the near end of the bar. In a fraction of a second, Buford knew Levine had taken pellets in the face, and that Grady was hit in the shoulder. The door behind him had a six-inch hole in it.

Those sitting at the bar, who were spared by the first resounding blast, weren't as lucky with the second. It followed only seconds later, ripping into shoulders and faces. Both bartenders dove behind the bar. The girls and their companions stampeded to the open dance floor; some were holding their faces and screaming. With the two rounds of the double-barreled shotgun spent, Buford stood up with his magnum pointed.

"Drop the gun, Callie!" Buford shouted.

He watched as she fumbled inside her purse. When she brought out the revolver, Buford had run out of options. He fired twice in rapid succession. The place was a bedlam, and Buford hadn't realized the thrust of his actions. He saw a lone girl still seated at the bar. She was clutching her face and crying pitifully. He saw Grady rise with his gun clutched in his uninjured hand. Buford moved through the smoke and sprawled figures to the end of the bar. When he looked to the floor where Callie had fallen, a wave of nausea swept over him. Her eyes were staring straight up. Blood oozed from two gaping bullet holes in her forehead.

A muscle spasm sent tremors throughout his body. He looked to the ceiling to suppress a compulsion to retch. He filled his lungs with air, and turned away. He went to a girl seated on the floor behind a bar stool. She stared at him blankly, blood gushing from a deep shoulder wound. Buford got out his handkerchief, and pushed it against the wound with her other hand.

He moved to the girl who remained seated at the bar. Her face was clutched in her hands. Blood seeped between the fingers.

"My face!" she cried. "My God . . . my face!"

Buford forced the hands away and looked closely at the pellet punctures. "Get me a towel," he told the bartender, who was back on his feet.

Buford used the fresh bar towel to blot her face. "You're all right," he said reassuringly. "You'll live, and the marks won't even show." Leaving her with the towel against her face, Buford walked toward the entrance of the bar.

When Buford returned to his driveway, dawn had arrived. For a moment he leaned against the top of the car, his mind a turmoil of negative thought. He started toward the house, but changed his course. He walked to the backyard knoll that overlooked the catfish ponds. He stared into space.

Pauline had been watching from inside. When Buford failed to return to the house, she put on her bathrobe and went to him. He looked at her as she neared him, and tried to speak.

"I . . . I heard," she told him. She put her arms around him and held him close.

They stood together in their embrace for a long time. The sun rose in the eastern sky, and church bells began to acknowledge the arrival of Christmas day. Bells from a closer church joined in with a haunting rendition of "The First Noël."

Buford squeezed Pauline's arm, and looked at her. "Merry Christmas," he said.

Chapter Fourteen

"They've Killed My Wife!"

Perhaps it was his own conscience, but Buford anticipated severe punishment for killing Callie. At times he was able to rationalize his actions. After all she had fired point-blank at him and others, and she had certainly been guilty of at least one murder herself; the one he had seen personally. Prior to the shooting, Buford had often plotted a just comeuppance for the female criminal, but never had he expected to dole out her punishment personally. Shortly after the shooting, he handed over his badge to Grady Coker. He intended to assign Grady as temporary sheriff until a special election could be held. Grady and Obra finally convinced him that he should hold off.

As it turned out, there was no pressure for impeachment, nor was there any great furor over the unfortunate killing. Even the bar girls at the Green Lantern gave a fairly accurate account of the altercation. After a brief and unemotional inquest hearing, the shooting was deemed justifiable.

Although he had been absolved of all guilt, Buford still had to live with his own nightmares, and they didn't drift away as quickly as local discussion. This had been the first woman he had ever killed, and he vowed it would be the last . . . no matter what the circumstance.

With early spring breaking over southwest Tennessee, Buford managed to spend much more time on family outings. It was essential as a level to his other existence. It was also requisite to keep alive the strong family bonds that were so vital to his sanity. Nothing on earth was more important to him than Pauline and the children. His world revolved around them, and despite the detours his integrity dictated, every road led back to them. He wanted McNairy County to be free of blatant vice and corruption, and perhaps there was a degree of altruism in his attempt to make it that way, but he knew his real motivation was more personal. He wanted his home territory to be a wholesome and healthy place to rear his children, and for them to grow up and raise families of their own.

It was Mike who suggested the family picnic, and Buford was quick to second the motion. Pauline packed the lunch, and to add novelty to the occasion, Buford rigged the flatbed trailer on the back of the tractor. Pauline rode on it with the kids, and they laughed all the way to the most distant catfish pond. The tractor was parked beside an oak tree. Pauline spread the blanket on the new grass in its shade.

Under the command of sibling competition, the children ran to the pond with fish poles ready. It was important to each of them to be the winner of the first catch. Mike had his hook baited in moments, and Dwana was frustrated. But soon they were both seated on the dock with feet dangling in the water.

Buford started to settle down on the blanket for a brief rest before lunch, but he became aware of Pauline's side-glances. He grinned, and unstrapped his gun belt. After placing it on the nearby tractor seat, he gave her a kiss on the cheek. "Is that better?" he asked her.

"Much better," she said, wrapping his arms around her.

They had just settled down on the blanket, when a wail of jealousy came from Dwana. "Mike's got a fish already!" she complained loudly. "He gets everything first!"

Buford leaned over his shoulder toward them. "Patience, honey . . . patience."

A few moments later the sound of an approaching vehicle roused Buford from his daydreams. He stood up, and instinctively brought his hand where his gun had been. He watched pensively as the car came partway into the drive. Then it stopped and began to back up to the highway. When it pulled away, Buford sighed with relief and returned to the blanket. Pauline said nothing, and Buford didn't attempt an explanation. It was simply the way life had to be, at least now. He was confident, however, that such apprehension would eventually cease.

Some moments later, Pauline lay back with her head on his lap. She chewed a blade of grass. "We could have more days like this," she said, "if you weren't sheriff."

"Maybe in a small way my being sheriff makes days like this possible . . . for a lot of people."

"*Small* way?" Pauline said, stirring. "You've gambled your very life! And nobody's said as much as thank-you."

"I may be wrong. Maybe nobody really gives a darn. But the way things have been going, I feel the job's more important than I even realized in the beginning." After a pause: "I think we've broken their backs, Pauline. Like in a war . . . you win the big battle, and then it's just a matter of mopping up."

"I'm really proud of you, Buford," Pauline said, studying his upside-down face. "And I'm not so scared any more."

Buford removed the blade of grass from her mouth, framed her face in his hands, and kissed her on the lips. As the embrace started to become more meaningful, they became aware of childish giggling down by the pond. The activity under the oak tree had taken on more immediate importance to the children than the catfish contest. Smiling, Pauline relaxed the embrace.

The day had been pleasantly active for the children, who had caught more catfish than they wanted to clean, and had been restful and serene for Buford. There had been no conflict to mar the acquired holiday. When he and Pauline went to bed, Buford fell asleep immediately, not out of exhaustion but out of peace and contentment.

When the phone rang, Buford thought he was dreaming at first. It was still dark outside, but on the second ring he lifted the receiver next to the bed. "Hello," he said, using his hand to shield Pauline from the sound of his voice. "Who is this?"

After rubbing the sleep from his eyes, Buford lighted the bed lamp and jiggled the phone. He sat up then and dialed the operator. He asked where the call had come from, and who else was on that line. With her scant information absorbed, Buford got up and took off his pajama top. Pauline, he discovered, was wide awake.

"Who was it?" she asked.

"A party line down at Donald Springs," he told her. "Neighbor overheard someone planning to set up another still. I'll go down and read them the riot act. It'll save me the work of tearing it down. Go back to sleep, honey."

He turned off the bed lamp, grabbed his clothes, and went into the adjacent bathroom. Almost immediately, Pauline switched the light back on and got out of bed. "Buford," she called, "I'm going with you."

"You say something?" he said, opening the door.

"I'm wide awake," she said. "Grandma gets up early. I'll ask her to stay with the kids. I think it's time I found out how my husband earns his living."

Buford smiled and went back to his shaving.

Dawn was breaking when Buford and Pauline left the house. She was wearing his favorite skirt: the red and white cotton print. With it, she wore a crisp white blouse, and her hair was tied with a bright bandana. This was how she had dressed the day they returned home. Buford reached the car ahead of her and opened the door. "Ah, a breath of spring," he said, kissing her cheek as she got inside.

"The weather?" she said smiling.

"No," he said. "I'm talking about my bride."

As Buford sat beside her, Pauline tossed her sweater over the seat.

"Probably nothing but a false alarm," Buford said, as he started the car. "We'll wind up just taking a nice early morning drive."

"Good," she said. "You can buy me breakfast on the way back."

Within a half hour, they were driving over

the byways of a part of McNairy County Pauline had never seen. They rounded a picturesque curve and came upon a quaint red brick church with a white steeple. Pauline commented on its beauty, when they entered a road of red clay that sent up clouds of dust obscuring the view.

As they wound around the dust ladened curve beyond the clearing, a pair of sedans spun out from the church yard with a spray of gravel. The cars took pursuit after the black sheriff's cruiser.

Buford slowed down as he approached a plank-covered bridge. Pauline was immersed in the early morning beauty of the primitive countryside. "Oh, Buford," she said, reaching over to him. "What a perfectly beautiful day. Thank you for taking me along."

She leaned over the center console to kiss his cheek. With the distraction, Buford failed to see the cars grinding down from behind. They had gone only a few hundred yards past the bridge, over a section of straight road, when the cars closed in under their cover of dust. One of them drew alongside, and Buford gasped at the intrusion. As he drew his gun, he saw M-14 rifles aimed at him. He saw Buel Jaggers clearly, and Otie Doss . . . just as they began firing.

Bullets smashed through the windshield, then through the side of the car and the back. Pauline was struck several times. First she was dashed forward against the dashboard; a second barrage caught her, and her body spun in the seat. Finally, she was slapped against the door on her side, and slumped there, in a tangle of arms and legs.

Buford fired repeatedly at the first car until

the second one was broadside. He recognized Augie McCullah firing through one of the open windows. Buford felt the back window of his cruiser explode from the barrage of shots. He switched his magnum to his left hand and accelerated. The cruiser shot ahead of both cars and darted forward along the narrow road. As he drove, he tried repeatedly to lift Pauline from the corner, but she couldn't be budged. She lay tangled in a mass of blood, half on the seat, half off.

The car was hitting the hundred mark, but Buford could only think of Pauline. Finally, the speed took control. The car barrelled out of the lane into a gravel road. It slid over the shoulder, along a ploughed field, and dipped back across the shoulder into the road. It charged forward over a hillcrest until it was totally airborne. Then it slapped down to the gravel and began to skid. Buford fought the wheel with momentary flights of control, but the speed was too much. The car leaped off the road and finally skidded and swerved to a stop in an open field.

Buford scrambled out of the car and ran around to Pauline's door. After a momentary gaze up the hill, he opened the door and frantically reached for Pauline. Gently, he lifted her into his arms, his voice making strange sobbing sounds that even he could hear. "Oh, God, God . . . Pauline!"

Her hair was drenched in blood, the bullet holes were clearly visible in her face and forehead. The red and white skirt was all red now. So was her starched, white blouse.

Buford started to carry her off. He didn't

know where. His mind was spinning; he was hysterical. Then, in a wild clump of machinery and steel the two cars bounced into the field. They swerved on either side of Buford and Pauline, spraying automatic weapon fire as they sped. Buford vainly attempted to shield Pauline with his body. He was hit again and again. One burst tore off his jaw and shattered his cheeks. The force of an opposite blast drove him sideways against the car. Pauline dropped from his grasp, and his body was caught in a mad pirouette that brought him sprawling at the front of the car. The attackers sped out of the field and back onto the highway.

It was silent . . . so deadly silent. A gurgling sound could be heard, and Buford looked around in a daze to identify it. He could see then it was coming from him; coming from the gaping hole that once was his mouth. Only seconds had passed, but it seemed like hours. *Pauline* . . . he remembered.

Slowly he rose to a knee and gazed at the forlorn and tangled body beside the car. He crawled to her, drew her into his arms, and staggered to his feet. In his panic, the most important goal was to stop her bleeding, but how? He placed his fingers over the quarter-sized holes to stop the blood from flowing. He tried to speak, to reassure her, but only moans and gasps came from his throat.

Buford held Pauline against him as he slumped on the car seat. He tried to work the mike switch, and was finally successful, but he couldn't speak. Propping Pauline against him with an elbow, he used the other hand to pull his sagging bone and marrow together. "Sheriff . . . help. Sheriff . . . help."

Grady's voice came up. "I can't understand you . . . is this you, Buford?"

In desperation, Buford loaded Pauline into the car, and staggered to the driver's side. He got in, and managed to start the engine. By instinct he maneuvered the car back to the road. With his blood gushing from his wounds, he somehow negotiated the several-mile distance to Highway 57. He swerved to a stop, straddling the center divider. He ran around the car to Pauline, and sat on the pavement with her in his arms while he attempted to use the radio.

The radio crackled with Grady's voice. "Where are you?" he asked.

Buford once more manipulated his jaw to allow the forming of words. "Highway . . . Fifty . . . seven. Fifty . . . seven."

"Fifty-seven?" Grady repeated. "Did you say fifty-seven?"

Buford dropped the microphone, and cradled Pauline in his arms. He gazed to the treeline and saw the white steeple emerging from the trees. "Oh, God," he moaned. "Don't let her die . . . please God. . . ."

A lifetime later, Buford heard the distant wail of sirens. Then they were upon him. He heard Grady say: "Get an ambulance down here! Highway Fifty-seven near Brant's Lane. For God's sake, make it fast!"

They attempted to remove Pauline from his grasp, but Buford wouldn't allow it. He held her tightly, continually trying to plug up the holes in her head. He would only release her when the ambulance arrived, and she was given a stretcher. Buford placed her limp form on the sheet with great care. He stood swaying as they rolled her away.

Obra touched his shoulder. "Please Sheriff. We've got to get you to the hospital."

"No," Buford mumbled. Then he fell to his face against the pavement, unconscious for the first time.

When the attendants carried him off, Obra turned and walked to his cruiser. He paused at the door for a moment. Then with a mournful wail of pent-up emotion, he slammed his fist into the window. When it failed to break, he struck it again and again. Grady and a pair of other deputies leaped on him and pulled him aside. His fists were mangled into red pulp. Now, with his outlet removed, Obra broke down and cried like a child.

Chapter Fifteen

The Challenge of Tomorrow

It was nearly eight hours later when the stretcher was wheeled from the operating room. The halls were lined with reporters from as far away as Nashville. Interspersed among the straining mass of newsmen and television equipment was a contingent from the Tennessee Bureau of Investigation, led by Lester Dickens. Grandpa Pusser was there, standing alone by the door, and so were Grady and Obra. Obra's hands were bandaged like mittens.

On the stretcher, being pushed by two attendants, was a head and face totally encased in a plaster cast. Holes had been cut for the eyes and the mouth. It could have been almost anyone, but the size of the form identified the patient as Buford.

A cameraman moved in close for a blinding final shot, as the stretcher headed into a corridor. "Get out of here," Grady said, giving the reporter a shove.

When the halls were cleared, Lester Dickens approached Obra. "The Governor's turned over his entire investigative staff to work on this case," he said. "Shall we start?"

Obra stared into a pair of very blue eyes. "You're a little late, aren't you?" Obra said.

Seeing the men bristle, Grady interceded, "We'll drive you to where they ambushed him."

It was after dark when Grady and Obra returned with the TBI investigators. They entered the lobby of the hospital, but Grady stopped them short. He saw a small blond-haired figure enter the building behind them. The child, red-faced from crying, was Mike Pusser. He carried his Christmas shotgun and a box of shells.

"What's going on?" asked one of the investigators.

"It's okay," said Grady. "That's Buford's boy. He's here to look after his dad."

They followed at a safe distance as Mike moved down the hallway. When Mike neared Buford's room, he encountered Grandpa, who had been leaning wearily against the wall. Grandpa started to intercept the boy, but thought better of it. He watched silently as Mike entered the restricted room.

The others joined Grandpa outside the room. Grady said to Obra: "If I get a shotgun from the car, are you up to standing guard? You take a shift in the hall here. I'll put another man outside the building."

Obra silently agreed.

Inside the room, a nurse was adjusting the plasma bottle above Buford's bed. She was startled by Mike's entrance, but watched quietly as he placed the shells on a night table. He then drew up a chair and sat in it, with his shotgun resting across his knees. Tears welled in his eyes as he watched his silent father.

Buford slowly opened his palm to Mike. Mike grasped it and Buford squeezed the small hand tightly. Quietly Obra, Grady and the TBI men entered the room. Dickens smiled at Mike, and moved closer to Buford.

"Pardon me, Sheriff," said Dickens, "but

146

we'd like to ask you some questions if you're up to it." Buford slowly nodded. "We picked up more than a hundred and twenty-five shells on the road. How many men were in the cars?"

Buford lifted his hands to indicate six or seven.

"Surely you recognized one or two of them?" Dickens said.

Buford didn't stir.

"Everybody in the capital isn't on the take," Dickens said, with understanding. "We're only trying to help. Don't you trust us?"

Buford shook his head negatively.

Dickens started to form another phrase, but changed his mind. He shrugged his shoulders and walked out of the room. The other TBI men followed. In their absence, Obra moved to the bed.

"Do you know who they are, Sheriff?" Obra asked.

Buford stared first at Obra and then to Grady. He nodded affirmatively.

Nobody could recall a gathering of this size in McNairy County. The church was filled to overflowing, and the lawn and streets were lined with friends and strangers. Police units from five states were parked intermittently along the village street. All businesses were closed for the funeral.

After the casket was carried to the waiting hearse, the fire bell began to toll. The procession moved slowly through the streets to the hillside cemetery. It became several blocks long as the march continued. Directly behind the hearse were Buford's mother and father, with Dwana and Mike. Behind them were all the deputies of McNairy County, with the exception of Obra. Several visiting deputies marched solemnly on either side of the hearse.

As the procession moved beyond the downtown business section, a lone sheriff's cruiser moved toward the stragglers along the deserted street. Slowly it inched forward among the mourners until it caught up with the hearse. Obra was driving the car. Buford sat beside him, his head encased in the white plaster cast.

Buford got out of the car in front of the volunteer fire station, where a Boy Scout stood before the giant bell, tolling it in measured cadence. Buford moved between Dwana and Mike, taking each by the hand. Mike walked tall beside his father over the final yards to the cemetery.

The woods grew to the very boundary of Hillside Cemetery. There was a sweeping view of the village and surrounding hills. In the distance the bell continued to toll, as the minister said his brief words at the gravesite. After their utterance, Buford leaned down for a handful of earth, which he silently threw over the casket. Mike matched his father's action, and then Dwana. Buford took the hands of both children and moved through the crowd.

When Buford joined Obra at the cruiser, he turned to his son. "Mike," he said. "Go get me a big stick."

Mike looked at him quizzically for a moment, but then ran into the woods.

A few minutes later, Buford was alone in the cruiser, speeding along Highway 45. The siren was blaring, the flasher was on. Buford drove with his left hand. He held an M-16 in the right. The big stick, delivered by Mike, was in the seat beside him.

As Buford came over a hill, he could see the deserted parking lot of the Lucky Spot. But it wasn't entirely deserted. He could see two figures fumbling with the lock at the front door. Buford increased his speed until there was no space left on the accelerator. As he bore into the parking lot, he saw Buel Jaggers standing in the doorway. He had an M-14 raised and aimed toward the cruiser. Buford started to stop, but changed his mind. He drove in a direct line with the poised weapon and the man holding it. As the last moment, Jaggers looked up from the gun and tried to flee, but there was no time. The car plunged into the Lucky Spot, taking wall, doors, chairs, and tables with it. It came to a steaming halt just in front of the bar. Jaggers was somewhere beneath the doors on which the car was resting.

For a moment Buford sat in the car, stunned by the impact. Blood began to trickle from the openings in his cast. He shook his head, took a long breath of air, and fumbled for the door latch. He got out, carrying the M-16 in one hand and the big stick in the other.

Augie watched fearfully from his vantage point near the gaming room. Now, with Buford still on the move, his fear turned to terror. He stood in the doorway petrified, unable to run, unable to reach for a weapon. Buford stalked him on unsteady legs, mumbling under his breath. He lashed out at Augie with the stick, knocking him into a sprawling heap across an upturned bar stool. Buford raised the stick

149

again, this time with full strength. He held it over his head for a long moment, and finally let the stick drop to the floor.

Buford took two steps and fell to his knees. He arose again but stumbled, the M-16 sliding along the floor. Again he stood up and staggered to the parking lot outside. There he slumped to his knees in exhaustion. He tried to lift himself again, but was distracted. He was alerted by the sound of a siren. He looked to the highway to see a sheriff's car approaching. It was being driven by Grady with Obra riding beside him. But what puzzled Buford more than that was the stream of cars behind the cruiser. There were dozens of them of all sizes and vintage.

Buford eased to a sitting position as the cars stopped. He saw angry townspeople get out of their family vehicles, and run into the Lucky Spot. They began throwing the furniture and equipment outside into the lot.

Obra came to Buford. "Come on, Sheriff," he said with a hand under his arm. "Let's get back to the hospital."

Buford tried to speak, but was unable. Grady helped Obra lift him to his feet.

"We'll get them, Buford," Grady assured. "We'll get every last one of them."

Buford was gently eased into the back seat of the cruiser. With his cast smeared with blood, Buford turned his head to watch his neighbors at their work. They had a huge pile accumulated now. He saw a dice table, slot machines, bar stools and dozens of cases of whiskey. Before the car began its trip back to the hospital, Buford saw someone set the fire.

The flames rose and enveloped the mound of materials. Soon everything would be returned to ashes.

Buford gazed out the window without conscious thought. He felt no elation in his moment of conquest; the price had been too high. At this moment he felt neither pain, grief nor sorrow. It was a kind of limbo—a recess from reality. But there would come tomorrow when all the truths must be weighed and sifted. And he would meet the challenge. That was how it had to be with Buford the Wild Bull.

"Pauline," he beckoned, without thinking.

The wail of the siren canceled his call.

THE BEST IN READING
FROM PINNACLE BOOKS!

THE CHINESE CONNECTION by William Crawford. Here is an absorbing tale of drug running and murder in the Southwest, with strange ties to the Far East. With a unique and richly conceived cast of characters, it reveals a world of which *The French Connection* offered a first hint. For these are people who would stop at nothing to attain their goals—for whom violence, sex, bribery and assassination are only way stations on the road to the big money and the power that money will buy. It's up to one honest man—a man not afraid to kill—to stop the scheme before a chain is forged which cannot be broken. A shattering Pinnacle original.   **P232—95¢**

MICKEY COHEN: MOBSTER by Ed Reid. Finally—the brutal truth about a well-known gangster! Mickey Cohen is alive and well and living in Los Angeles, the last of the big-time mobsters still breathing. This is a story that Mickey Cohen would rather *not* have told, but a story that can no longer be kept secret. For it is truth—truth sometimes stranger than any fiction can be—about a man who has always been larger than life, who is part of the social history of our time. He is a member of the Mafia— the Jewish Mafia—a group that has been largely ignored in the many Mafia books. He is a man who has lived hard and lived flamboyantly. Right now, he's down, but don't ever count him out. Not until the end. An illustrated Pinnacle original.
                                                          P257—$1.25

MINDINAO PEARL by Alan Caillou. An exciting novel of high adventure and intrigue. David Calib, young and accustomed to big city life, is sent by his father to find a man named Smith, who has disappeared with stolen money. Smith is on the island of Pangalu, in the South Seas, hiding in the jungle because he has stolen more than money. He has a treasure in pearls, among them a beautiful black pearl, taken from the two brothers with whom he had been partners. The brothers—both violent-tempered—suspect that Calib is an accomplice of Smith and plan to kill him. But he escapes with their lovely sister, Andree, and they begin the deadly game of hide and seek—from her brothers and from Smith. The chase will keep you gripping the book until the last suspenseful page. P238—95¢

VIZZINI! by Sal Vizzini, with Oscar Fraley and Marshall Smith. The secret lives of our most successful narc! Sal Vizzini may die because this book has been written. He was formerly an undercover agent for the Federal Bureau of Narcotics—an assignment which took him to Naples, where he became a "friend" of exiled Mafia chieftain Charles "Lucky" Luciano; to Burma, where he outwitted a Communist gun-running ring; and to Atlanta, Georgia, where he posed as a con in a Federal pen. He was shot three times, knifed twice, beaten nearly to death, and had several contracts put out by the Mafia to kill him. Many of the men now in jail will learn for the first time who put them there. P226—$1.25

MIND OUT by Diana Carter. A provocative novel about a far-out communal group. The "Cerebralists" are a group who entice young, alienated, often rather confused people to join their strange cult. They are then forced to sign over all their property. But to whom? No one knows the leader. He communicates with his members through strange codes and supervises them by closed-circuit TV. There are strange, mind-bending initiation rites, which some do not survive and which leave others in a permanent childlike state. Giselle Baker is the child of a famous, but aging, French movie actress. She is induced to join the group by the first man she meets. What happens to her will frighten and fascinate you. A book no one will be able to put down. P220—95¢

SILENT SQUADRON by Peter Leslie. An exciting World War II submarine adventure. The stage is set for taut drama when a secret Nazi U-boat nest is discovered in neutral Ireland. It's in a perfect defensive position, with a rocky coastline and high smashing waves to prevent an infiltration or attack. But fourteen men get the mission to eliminate the base. How can they do it? One way is to bomb the hideout, but Ireland is a neutral country and the Irish are not aware of the real purpose of the German facility. It is a political dilemma and a do-or-die assignment. Gripping suspense, action that never lets up, an explosive climax and superb writing make for a smashing novel. P192—95¢

NOWHERE ON EARTH by Michael Elder. Here is superior science fiction with the threat of reality, for this is the odyssey of one very ordinary man, fighting for his family in a world in which rebellion, either in thought or deed, is not tolerated. His story is both engrossing and frightening—it is a story that is just around the corner from today. Roger Barclay is hunting for his wife and newborn daughter, who have disappeared from a maternity hospital. No one will answer his anguished questions, so he turns to an underground group, led by a mysterious revolutionary, for help. What he finds will surprise you. **P157N—95¢**

SIEGE AND SURVIVAL: THE ODYSSEY OF A LENINGRADER by Elena Skrjabina. A diary of one of the most devastating sieges in history. During the siege of Leningrad which began on September 8, 1941, nearly one-and-one-half million people died —of hunger, of cold, of disease, from German bullets and bombs. Elena Skrjabina survived. She endured. This book is a record of that experience, and it has been acclaimed by critics everywhere. *Publishers Weekly* said that it is "written in unadorned but eloquent prose that is remarkably affecting." *Bestsellers* said "It is human." **P199N—95¢**

HERO IN THE TOWER by Hans Hellmut Kirst. A spellbinding story of power, psychosis, and murder! Take a bestselling novel, a top author, critical acclaim, and what do you get. Pinnacle's big new novel—HERO IN THE TOWER. The hero is German Army Captain Karl Ludwig Hein, who is the head of antiaircraft Battery No. 3, and who is typical of the officers of the German Army of World War II—both the corrupters and those they so easily corrupt. This novel reveals all the special gifts that have distinguished Kirst's previous work and that have made him the unparalleled chronicler of Germany under Hitler's Reich. It is his most ambitious and powerful novel since the worldwide bestseller, *Night of the Generals.* **P145—$1.50**

ESCAPE FROM PRAGUE by Brian Cleeve. A TV journalist plunged into a nightmare of brutality! To read the first paragraph of this novel is to be plummeted into the world of ruthless savagery that still exists in certain parts of Europe, behind the Iron Curtain. There can be no escape from such a world except by illegal methods—by risking one's life in a final bid for freedom. Tony Brett's exciting escape story has depths of characterization that make for high adventure and suspense—plus a shattering chase that will leave you on the edge of your chair! Here is one man against the Communists, in a battle for his life.

THE FIRE FIGHTERS by Jack Pearl. An insider novel. What it is really like to be a fireman! Larry Hughes is a fireman, a man who puts his life on the line every time the station bell rings. He never knows just what is going to happen. It may be just as well. He works in a large city. Sometimes he has to fight people as well as fires—for the right to put out the fire, for a right to another day as a fireman. Another day that may be his last. He's watched his friends die, knowing he cannot help them. Putting out fires which were started because someone was bored, or sick, or angry. Here is a book that tells it as it is—the exciting, dangerous, suspense-filled world of the fireman. A blazing book.

BOUNTY HUNT AT BALLARAT by Clayton Matthews. A western in the best hard-hitting tradition! When Clint Devlin rode into Ballarat, he thought he was coming to avenge the brutal murder of his girl friend's father. And he thought that the murderer was a woman. He was wrong. But it took a while to find out the truth. And the truth surprised everyone. Especially Clint Devlin. Here is a tense Western drama, with just a little something added. It's got all the spine-tingling excitement you readers are looking for, the atmosphere of the Old West, and romantic interest too!

THE CONSPIRATOR WHO SAVED THE ROMANOVS by Gary Null. The amazing story of Nicholas and Alexandra's escape. At last the true story of how the royal family of Russia was saved from death in 1918. Here are authenticated documents, illustrations, a story stranger than fiction and intriguing in every sense of the word! A bestselling novel and a colossal motion picture have brought interest in the royal pair to greater heights than ever. But no one ever suspected that an anonymous—until now—jeweler was responsible for the plot to keep the royal family alive.

VENDETTA by Joseph Gilmore. A book about a tough cop looking for revenge! What happens when a tough but tender-hearted cop finds his wife—the most important person in his life—murdered by a dose of bad heroin. What happens when he tries to bring those men to justice, by the book, and meets failure at every turn because of judicial red tape and loopholes in the law? His sense of duty to the law changes to a sense of duty of another sort: a duty to keep others from dying unnecessarily because of the drug traffic. The deal he offers the Mafia bosses is a deal they can't refuse—instant death in the form of a bullet in the brain. The suspense never lets up; the action is unceasing; and the questions Alex Braley—cop—asks, have still not been answered.   P170N—95¢

STAND BY TO DIE by A. V. Sellwood. The heroic story of a lone, embattled WW II ship. It was a small Yangtse river steamer, manned by a makeshift crew of fugitives. She sailed from war-torn Singapore to do battle with the armed might of a Japanese fleet. It was an epic naval action. Heroism was the order of the day. There were no lean British cruisers to divert Japanese guns, there were no RAF planes to provide air cover. Just one bullet-riddled tub that wouldn't say die! The story could have been lost forever, as it has been for many years, had not A. V. Sellwood pieced together the almost unbelievable story of "the most decorated small ship in the navy."   P171N—95¢

SIBERIA 10 by Clark Howard. A searing novel of brutality and racial tension! There are riots in a marine prison stockade. It is alleged that the riots are being caused by the guards' brutality, with racial overtones. The white guards are persecuting the black prisoners; the black guards are doing the same to the white prisoners. If something isn't done quickly, the camp will literally go up in smoke. Hannon finds it to be his most difficult mission in a long battle-scarred career. Here is a novel as timely as today's headlines with a hero that all readers will find compellingly fascinating. Can whites and blacks work together and live together without killing each other? Even when they're trained killers? That is the thrust of the story, the savage story.
                                                        P169Z—$1.25

CHRIST ON TRIAL by Roger Dixon. Lee Harrison, a TV producer who has seen many better days, decides that his swansong will be a modern day trial of Jesus of Nazareth. The court will hear all the facts, the events that occurred 1,973 years ago, and will attempt to prove beyond a shadow of a doubt the guilt or innocence of Jesus. Millions of Americans will witness the proceedings on their television sets—will decide for themselves whether the accused could have been the Son of God. The TV play—and the book about it—has a surprise ending that no one, not even the producers, directors and actors could have foreseen.   P139—$1.50

THE KARAMANOV EQUATIONS by Marshall Goldberg. An extraordinary novel of international intrigue! Hippocratic Oath or Pledge of Allegiance? The wrong choice could destroy the world! A noted Russian scientist, who is on the verge of a breakthrough discovery that will make his country impregnable to missile attack and master of the world, has a heart attack. The best doctor available is an American who has been pioneering new techniques of surgery. The Soviets hope to persuade the American that the patient is an insignificant Frenchman. A taut drama—supercharged with suspense and crackling with tension.
                                                P158—$1.25

LAST CONTRACT by Clark Howard. A first-rate adventure—brutal and compelling! George Trevor. Mafia hitman. He thought he had a slick, bulletproof plan; he'd had seventeen years of experience in surviving. He was forty-one and looked it, but that didn't matter to him. Efficiency did. It kept him alive. Actually, he wasn't as uncomplicated as he seemed. It had taken a lot—the Korean War and the Red Chinese torture, for one—to turn him into a fierce and ruthless man. A man who wanted out. Remember his name. You won't forget his story.
                                                P161—95¢

BRANNON by Daniel T. Streib. A gut-wrenching novel of brutality and revenge. Brannon, a brash young soldier in 1952, is fresh from the wars and passing through the town of Timberland, a mill town owned and ruled by one Adam Ward. His good looks are exceeded only by his confidence and he overcomes the daughter of the mill owner. Brannon is caught and beaten by the men of the town. But more, his vital young manhood is cut off at its peak! And just what does a man do when this most unspeakable and inhuman thing happens to him? It takes years, but Brannon returns. And an entire town is the object of his seething revenge.   P155—95¢

If these books are not available in your bookstore, just write to PINNACLE BOOKS, P.O. Box 4347, Grand Central Station, New York, N.Y. 10017, enclosing the retail price, plus 10¢ to cover mailing and handling costs for each book ordered.